Eyewitness
DINOSAUR

Magnolia flower

Armored *Polacanthus* skin

Rock fragment with iridium deposit

Corythosaurus

Tyrannosaurus coprolite (fossil dropping)

Megalosaurus jaw

Troodon embryo

Eyewitness
DINOSAUR

Megalosaurus tooth

Written by
DAVID LAMBERT

Kentrosaurus

Ammonite mold

Ammonite cast

LONDON, NEW YORK,
MELBOURNE, MUNICH, AND DELHI

Gila monster

Consultant Dr. David Norman

Senior editor Rob Houston
Editorial assistant Jessamy Wood
Managing editors Julie Ferris, Jane Yorke
Managing art editor Owen Peyton Jones
Art director Martin Wilson
Associate publisher Andrew Macintyre
Picture researcher Louise Thomas
Production editor Melissa Latorre
Production controller Charlotte Oliver
Jacket designers Martin Wilson,
Johanna Woolhead
Jacket editor Adam Powley

DK DELHI

Editor Kingshuk Ghoshal
Designer Govind Mittal
DTP designers Dheeraj Arora, Preetam Singh
Project editor Suchismita Banerjee
Design manager Romi Chakraborty
Production manager Pankaj Sharma
Head of publishing Aparna Sharma

Iguanodon hand

Troodon

First published in the United States in 2010 by
DK Publishing
375 Hudson Street, New York, New York 10014

10 11 12 13 14 10 9 8 7 6 5 4 3 2

175403—12/09

A catalog record for this book is available from
the Library of Congress.

ISBN 978-0-7566-5810-6 (Hardcover)
ISBN 978-0-7566-5811-3 (Library Binding)

Color reproduction by MDP, UK, and Colourscan, Singapore
Printed and bound by Toppan Printing Co. (Shenzhen) Ltd, China

Discover more at
www.dk.com

Ankylosaur scute
(bony plate)

Oviraptor egg

Contents

Ankylosaurus

What were the dinosaurs?

LONG AGO, STRANGE BEASTS roamed the world. Some grew as big as a barn, others were smaller than a hen. Some walked on four legs, others on two. Some were fierce hunters, others were peaceful plant-eaters. These backboned land animals are called dinosaurs. Dinosaur means "terrible lizard," and like lizards, dinosaurs were reptiles. But instead of sprawling, they walked upright, and some dinosaurs had feathers rather than scaly skin. In chilly air, instead of dozing like a lizard, some dinosaurs could stay active by generating their own body heat. The dinosaurs ruled Earth for 160 million years—flourishing on land more successfully than any other group of backboned animals. Then 65 million years ago, they mysteriously died out, except for one group—the dinosaurs that we call birds.

Opening in skull in front of eye reduced the weight of the skull

Neck with S-shaped curve

Hole between bones of lower jaw helped to lighten the skull

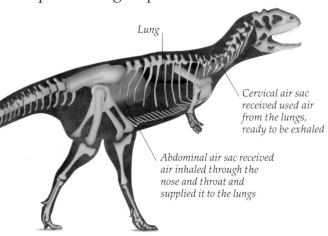

Lung

Cervical air sac received used air from the lungs, ready to be exhaled

Abdominal air sac received air inhaled through the nose and throat and supplied it to the lungs

A BREATH OF FRESH AIR
Unlike modern reptiles, some dinosaurs, including *Majungatholus*, had air sacs connected to their lungs, just as birds do. As in birds, the sacs acted like bellows, pushing a continuous flow of fresh air one way through the lungs. This breathing method is much more efficient than that of mammals. In mammals, some stale air gets mixed with fresh air in every breath.

FOSSIL FEATHERS
The fuzzy brown fringes around the skeleton of this fossil *Microraptor* are traces of feathers. Feathered dinosaurs had big advantages over those with scaly skin. *Microraptor's* feathers helped to keep this small predatory dinosaur warm in cold weather. Long showy feathers probably helped the males to attract mates. And when *Microraptor* jumped off a tree with its feathered arms outstretched, its leap became a long glide.

Head of femur (thigh bone) points inward to fit into socket between the hip bones, helping to keep the limb erect

WALKING TALL
The limb bones of dinosaurs show that they walked as mammals do, with legs erect underneath the body, not stuck out sideways as in lizards. The sprawling limbs of a lizard limit the expansion of the lungs when running, so the lizard must make breathing stops. The upright dinosaur did not have to stop to breathe when on the move. Also, the limbs of many dinosaurs could support bodies as heavy as a truck. Like those of most dinosaurs, the hind limbs of *Tyrannosaurus* had high ankles and narrow feet. *Tyrannosaurus* walked on its toes, which helped it to move quickly.

Homo sapiens, or fully modern humans, appeared only around 200,000 years ago

THE AGE OF DINOSAURS

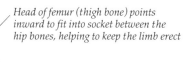

250 mya	200 mya	145 mya	65 mya	today
Triassic	Jurassic	Cretaceous		
	MESOZOIC ERA		CENOZOIC ERA	

A TIME BEFORE HUMANS
The Age of Dinosaurs lasted from about 230 million to 65 million years ago (mya). It spans most of the geological era known as the Mesozoic, which is divided into the Triassic, Jurassic, and Cretaceous periods. Other than birds, all dinosaurs died out long before the first humans appeared on Earth.

REPTILE RELATIONS
Elasmosaurus was the longest-known plesiosaur, one of a group of marine reptiles from the Mesozoic Era. It grew to as long as 46 ft (14 m). Other groups of large marine reptiles from this time include mosasaurs and ichthyosaurs. None of these was a dinosaur. They were from a different part of the reptile family tree.

Extremely long neck supported by 72 cervical vertebrae (neck bones)

Flipper-shaped limb

Upright hind limb

Thumblike digit allowed the hand to grasp

Hand with three main digits

Green, scaly skin

Sprawling leg

Weight-bearing toe

DINOSAUR FEATURES
Paleontologists—scientists who study fossils—helped to create this restoration of the meat-eating dinosaur *Monolophosaurus*. Like all dinosaurs this fearsome predator stood upright thanks to the construction of its hip joints. It was bipedal, walking only on its hind limbs, its heavy tail balancing its upper body. Like many bipedal dinosaurs, *Monolophosaurus*'s third digits (fingers) could twist a little to face the other two digits, forming grasping hands.

Hingelike ankle braced hind limb

TERRIBLE LIZARDS?
Dinosaurs were very unlike typical modern reptiles, such as this basilisk lizard. A basilisk is cold-blooded, meaning it relies on heat from the Sun for body warmth. But evidence of some dinosaurs' birdlike lungs and feathers suggests they were warm-blooded, maintaining constant body temperatures with internal body heat. Unlike modern reptiles, they probably had a high-energy lifestyle like birds and mammals.

Different designs

PALEONTOLOGISTS DIVIDE DINOSAURS INTO two groups, according to how their hip bones are arranged. Most saurischians had hip bones like a lizard's and were two-legged, meat-eating theropods, or four-legged, plant-eating sauropods. The ornithischians had hip bones like a bird's and were plant-eaters. They included two-legged ornithopods, as well as plated, armored, and horned dinosaurs, which were all four-legged. Bony plates or spikes ran along the backs of stegosaurs, or plated dinosaurs, and bony body armor protected the ankylosaurs, or armored dinosaurs. Ceratopsians, or horned dinosaurs, bore horns on their heads and bony frills over their necks. The family tree on pages 64–65 shows how all these dinosaurs were related.

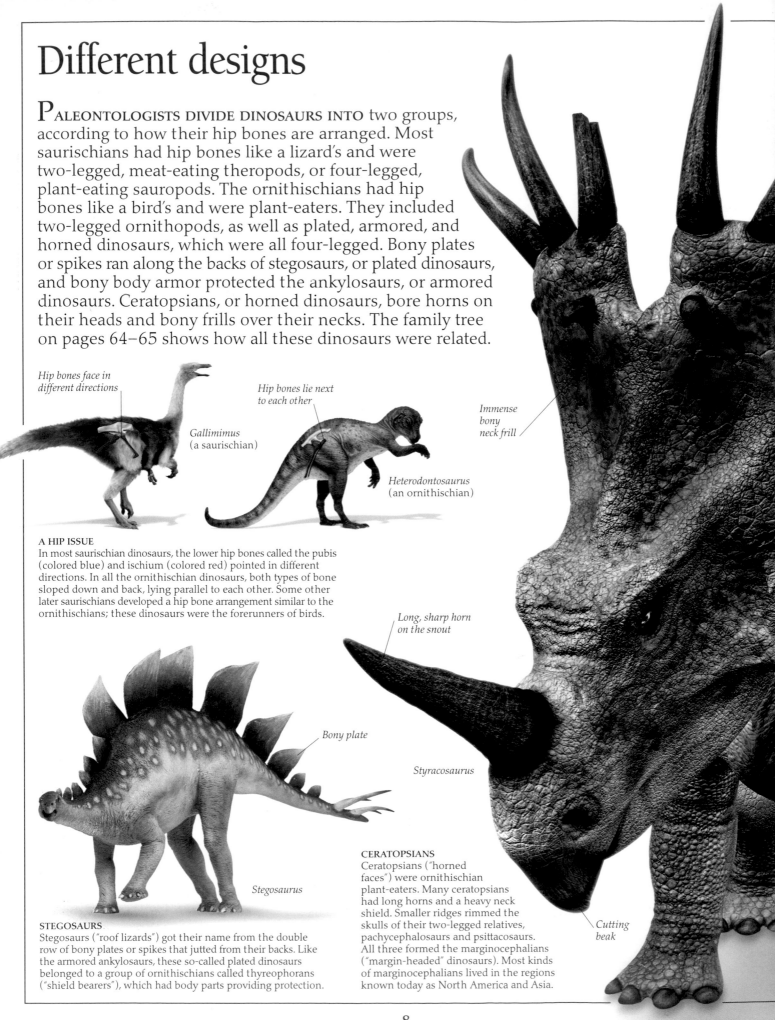

Hip bones face in different directions

Hip bones lie next to each other

Gallimimus (a saurischian)

Heterodontosaurus (an ornithischian)

Immense bony neck frill

A HIP ISSUE
In most saurischian dinosaurs, the lower hip bones called the pubis (colored blue) and ischium (colored red) pointed in different directions. In all the ornithischian dinosaurs, both types of bone sloped down and back, lying parallel to each other. Some other later saurischians developed a hip bone arrangement similar to the ornithischians; these dinosaurs were the forerunners of birds.

Long, sharp horn on the snout

Bony plate

Styracosaurus

Stegosaurus

CERATOPSIANS
Ceratopsians ("horned faces") were ornithischian plant-eaters. Many ceratopsians had long horns and a heavy neck shield. Smaller ridges rimmed the skulls of their two-legged relatives, pachycephalosaurs and psittacosaurs. All three formed the marginocephalians ("margin-headed" dinosaurs). Most kinds of marginocephalians lived in the regions known today as North America and Asia.

Cutting beak

STEGOSAURS
Stegosaurs ("roof lizards") got their name from the double row of bony plates or spikes that jutted from their backs. Like the armored ankylosaurs, these so-called plated dinosaurs belonged to a group of ornithischians called thyreophorans ("shield bearers"), which had body parts providing protection.

Bony spike jutting from neck frill

SAUROPODS

Sauropods were gigantic saurischians with long necks and tails. The largest were the most massive animals of any kind that ever walked on Earth. Along with their early and mostly smaller relatives, prosauropods, the sauropods formed a group of long-necked plant-eaters called sauropodomorphs. These spread to all parts of the world and lived as far south as present-day Antarctica.

Immensely long neck

Whiplike tail

Barosaurus

ORNITHOPODS

Ornithopods were plant-eaters that first appeared in the Jurassic Period. Early kinds were small and fast enough to outrun big meat-eaters. Later ones included bulky _Muttaburrasaurus, Iguanodon,_ and the hadrosaurs (duck-billed dinosaurs). These animals hurried on their hind limbs, but often ambled on all fours. The largest lived in the northern continents.

Bony bump on head

Sharp and horny beak

Heavy tail

Pillarlike leg

Muttaburrasaurus

Forelimb used as a foot

Armored bands

ANKYLOSAURS

Ankylosaurs were a group of armored ornithischians. Their four sturdy legs supported a barrel-shaped body. Some kinds, including _Euoplocephalus,_ had a tail that ended in a bony club. Sharp shoulder spikes protected others.

Bony tail club

Euoplocephalus

Nose horn

Bladelike teeth

THEROPODS

Theropods ("beast feet") were carnivorous, or meat-eating, saurischians. Most had sharp teeth, and clawed toes on strong, birdlike feet. The theropods ranged from huge _Tyrannosaurus_ to feathered animals no larger than a pigeon, some of which were ancestors of modern birds.

Ceratosaurus

Triassic times

THE TRIASSIC PERIOD lasted from around 250 to 200 million years ago. It was the first part of the Mesozoic Era—often called the Age of Dinosaurs. At this time, a mighty ocean surrounded a single massive continent. Some parts of the land were hot, and others were warm. Deserts covered inland regions cut off from moist winds that blew in from the ocean. Flowering plants had yet to appear. Reptilelike ancestors of mammals and many kinds of prehistoric reptile thrived in these conditions. Among the reptiles were lizards, plant-eating rhynchosaurs, and the ancestors of crocodiles. The first dinosaurs appeared in the latter half of the Triassic—some fed on plants, while others ate reptiles and the mammals' ancestors. Above them flew the skin-winged pterosaurs, and other reptiles swam in shallow offshore seas.

THE TRIASSIC WORLD
In this period, all landmasses formed one supercontinent that spanned the globe (from pole to pole). Scientists call this Pangaea ("all Earth"). Surrounding Pangaea was a single ocean, with a great inlet called the Tethys Sea. One landmass allowed the spread of dinosaurs across the globe.

Pangaea

Tethys Sea

Tuft of grasslike leaves on a single, unbranched trunk

Pleuromeia plants

ANCIENT PLANTS
Where the ground was moist enough for vegetation, strange plants thrived alongside some that are familiar to us today. Bushy-topped *Pleuromeia* was an unbranched treelike plant no taller than a man. Early in the Triassic Period, it lined many coasts and riversides. Damp places were also home to ferns and horsetails. Drier regions suited other kinds of plants, such as ginkgoes, seed ferns, cycads, palmlike plants called cycadeoids, and tall conifers related to the monkey puzzle tree.

Fern frond

Leaves of a ginkgo tree

Desertlike region

DAWN OF THE DINOSAURS
The first dinosaurs were probably small meat-eaters that were bipedal (walking on two legs). Plant-eaters, both bipedal and quadrupedal (walking on all fours), appeared at the end of the Triassic. By then, there were already theropods, prosauropods, and sauropods—the main groups of saurischian dinosaurs. The only known ornithischian dinosaurs were small bipeds not belonging to any of the later groups.

HERRERASAURUS (228 MYA)
This bipedal hunter from Triassic Argentina is one of the earliest-known dinosaurs, perhaps predating the first theropods. It had a long tail that it used for balance while running.

Flexible neck

REPTILES TAKE FLIGHT
A flying reptile about 28 in (70 cm) long, *Eudimorphodon* was one of the earliest-known pterosaurs, which were relatives of dinosaurs. It had skin wings, toothy jaws, and a long, bony tail. *Eudimorphodon* flew over what is now north Italy about 210 million years ago, perhaps seizing small fish with its sharp teeth.

Elongated fourth finger supports the wing

Clawed finger

Wing made of skin

Bony tail

Beak for cropping plants

Armored back

Front teeth project forward

ARMORED SEA REPTILES
Placodus ("flat tooth") belonged to a group of reptiles called placodonts, one of several kinds of large reptiles living in Triassic seas. It was as long as a man. About 200 million years ago, this sprawling, short-necked creature plucked shellfish from rocks with its jutting front teeth, then crushed them using flat teeth in the roof of its mouth.

Fossil skull

Sprawling limb

Fur probably covered body

THE EMERGENCE OF MAMMALS
Mammals emerged in the Triassic Period, evolving from reptilelike ancestors. Small, shrewlike *Megazostrodon* lived in southern Africa as the Triassic Period was ending. This furry creature had almost all the features of a mammal. It would have snapped up insects and baby lizards but kept well clear of hungry dinosaurs. *Megazostrodon* probably spent the daytime hiding in a hole and only ventured out to hunt at night.

PLANT-EATING REPTILES
Several groups of giant reptile dominated Triassic wildlife before dinosaurs gradually replaced them. This beaked skull comes from *Hyperodapedon*, a piglike reptile with a big head and a squat, barrel-shaped body. It was one of the rhynchosaurs, a group of plant-eating reptiles that chopped up seed ferns with their teeth. *Hyperodapedon* was widespread 220 million years ago.

Mammal-like teeth of different shapes and sizes

PLATEOSAURUS (215 MYA)
This prosauropod grew up to 26 ft (8 m) long, but the bulky plant-eater supported itself on its hind limbs only. *Plateosaurus* might have roamed in herds and was widespread in Late Triassic Europe.

EOCURSOR (210 MYA)
A plant-eater slightly larger than a fox, *Eocursor* is the only Triassic ornithischian dinosaur for which fairly complete fossils have been found. *Eocursor* ran very fast and lived in Triassic South Africa.

COELOPHYSIS (208 MYA)
This theropod was longer than a man, but lighter. It had slim, pointed jaws and small, sharp teeth, and swallowed smaller creatures whole. Paleontologists found many of its skeletons in New Mexico.

Jurassic times

THE JURASSIC PERIOD lasted from around 200 to 145 million years ago. It formed the middle part of the Mesozoic Era and is sometimes called the Age of Giants because huge sauropod dinosaurs flourished at this time. By now the supercontinent Pangaea had begun to crack. Where a great rift split apart Earth's continental crust, the Atlantic Ocean formed and then widened, separating lands on either side. Moist winds from the seas could reach many inland regions, bringing rain to places that had once been deserts. It was warm everywhere. Plants began to grow in barren lands, providing food for new kinds of large and small plant-eating dinosaurs. Above these, pterosaurs shared the air with the first birds, descendants of small predatory dinosaurs. Early salamanders swam in lakes and streams, and Jurassic seas swarmed with big swimming reptiles. Many of these hunted fish that resembled some of those alive today.

THE JURASSIC WORLD
Pangaea broke up into a northern landmass called Laurasia and a southern landmass called Gondwana. But these smaller supercontinents soon started breaking up as well. Laurasia started to split into the northern continents of North America, Europe, and Asia. Gondwana began splitting into South America, Africa, India, Australia, and Antarctica.

Sprawling limb

Backbone

Broad skull

FIRST AMPHIBIANS
Frogs and salamanders as we know them today first appeared in the Jurassic Period. *Karaurus* is one of the earliest-known salamanders. Paleontologists discovered its remains in Late Jurassic rocks in Kazakhstan. Despite its age, *Karaurus's* fossil skeleton resembles those of salamanders that are alive today. About 8 in (20 cm) long, this small amphibian was a good swimmer. It probably lived in streams or pools, snapping up creatures such as snails and insects.

JURASSIC SEA REPTILES
Aside from its long, narrow jaws and vertical tail, *Ichthyosaurus* ("fish lizard") was shaped like a dolphin. It grew 6½ ft (2 m) long and swam fast, using its large eyes to spot the fish it hunted for food. Ichthyosaurs were one of several groups of large Jurassic reptile superbly adapted for life in the sea. They were not related to dinosaurs.

GIANTS AND BIRDS
During the Jurassic Period, the prosauropods died out, but sauropods and theropods flourished. Among them were the largest plant-eating and meat-eating land animals of the time, although some theropods from this period were feathered creatures no bigger than crows. The ornithopods, stegosaurs, and ankylosaurs all appeared in the Jurassic Period.

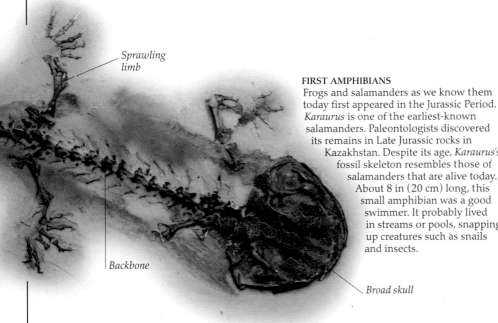

***SCELIDOSAURUS* (190 MYA)**
The ankylosaur *Scelidosaurus* was one of the earliest and most primitive armored dinosaur. As long as a mid-sized car, it lived in the northern landmass Laurasia.

***BARAPASAURUS* (190 MYA)**
Barapasaurus ("big-legged lizard") gets its name from a thigh bone 5½ ft (1.7 m) long. This sauropod had slim limbs and unusual hollows in its vertebrae (back bones). It grew 60 ft (18 m) long and lived in Jurassic India.

***GUANLONG* (160 MYA)**
Guanlong was one of the earliest members of the tyrannosauroid group of theropods. This crested dinosaur from China grew only 10 ft (3 m) long, but shared key features with *Tyrannosaurus*.

Long skull

Long neck

Wing made of skin

JURASSIC VEGETATION
The major types of plant at this time were those that had flourished in the Triassic Period. Gymnosperms included ginkgoes, monkey puzzle trees, and cycadeoids such as *Williamsonia*—a small, stumpy tree with palmlike fronds that sprouted from the top. Meadows of ferns, horsetails, and mosses carpeted damp soil. In drier areas, strips of forest lined the riverbanks. Flowering plants had not yet appeared.

Leaves of a monkey puzzle tree

Cycadlike leaves

Williamsonia plants

AGILE FLIERS
Jurassic pterosaurs such as *Pterodactylus* ("wing finger") had longer necks and skulls than their Triassic ancestors. Their short tails made them agile in the air. Many species of *Pterodactylus* lived in Africa and Europe, the largest with a wingspan of 8 ft (2.4 m). It is likely that these pterosaurs flew low over water, their sharp teeth seizing unsuspecting fish.

Powerful jaws

CROCODILE ANCESTOR
Protosuchus ("first crocodile") belonged to the same group of reptile as modern crocodiles and alligators—only remotely related to dinosaurs. But this animal had relatively longer and more agile legs and ran around on land. *Protosuchus* was a hunter the size of a large dog, armed with powerful jaws. It lived early in the Jurassic Period in present-day Arizona.

Short, stocky trunk

KENTROSAURUS (156 MYA)
Related to the more famous *Stegosaurus*, *Kentrosaurus* ("spiked lizard") bristled with paired narrow plates or spikes jutting from its neck, back, and tail. This plated dinosaur lived in East Africa.

SINRAPTOR (155 MYA)
Sinraptor lived in what is now a desert in northwest China. This big meat-eater, about 25 ft (7.6 m) long, was related to the better-known North American theropod *Allosaurus*.

ARCHAEOPTERYX (150 MYA)
The crow-sized bird *Archaeopteryx* had feathered wings and body but also had a theropod's teeth, claws, tail, and scaly legs. Fine-grained limestone rocks of southwest Germany preserve its fossil skeletons.

Cretaceous times

THE CRETACEOUS PERIOD lasted from 145 to 65 million years ago and closed the Mesozoic Era, marking the climax of the Age of Dinosaurs. Climates remained warm or mild, but great changes happened to our planet. Flowering plants began to replace older kinds, seas flooded low-lying lands, and continents split up and moved apart. As the landmasses separated, the dinosaurs that became cut off from one another adapted to different environments. In the late Cretaceous Period, there were probably more kinds of dinosaur than ever before.

THE CRETACEOUS WORLD
In the Cretaceous Period, the supercontinents Laurasia and Gondwana broke up completely. Their fragments gradually took on the shapes of the continents we know today. By the end of this period, most had drifted close to their present positions, but India had not yet docked with Asia. For a while, shallow seas overflowed stretches of low-lying land.

Upper part of trunk covered with leaves

FROM FOLIAGE TO FLOWERS
Early in the Cretaceous Period, plants such as conifers, cycads, and ferns still covered the land. A strange tree-fern called *Tempskya* was widespread in the northern continents. It had a false trunk made of stems surrounded by roots, with leaves that grew outward. Angiosperms, or flowering plants, appeared for the first time. They began to grow on open ground and spread out from the tropics, changing landscapes forever. Most early kinds of angiosperm were probably small and weedy, but some gave rise to shrubs and small trees. By the end of the Cretaceous Period, magnolias and other flowering trees had formed extensive forests.

Magnolia flower

Tempskya tree-fern forest

AN AGE OF DIVERSITY
Cretaceous dinosaurs included some of the most massive sauropods and theropods of all time. Theropods now also included an amazing variety of feathered birds and birdlike dinosaurs—some smaller than a sparrow, and others as large as an elephant. Stegosaurs had vanished, but the horned dinosaurs appeared, as did the largest ankylosaurs and ornithopods.

SAUROPELTA (115 MYA)
Twice the length of a large rhinoceros, *Sauropelta* was an ankylosaur that roamed the Early Cretaceous woodlands in western North America. Bony cones and studs guarded its back and tail against attack.

ALXASAURUS (110 MYA)
Alxasaurus ("Alxa lizard") from China's Alxa Desert was an early therizinosauroid—one of a group of pot-bellied, plant-eating theropods probably covered in feathery down.

STYRACOSAURUS (76.5 MYA)
A large horned dinosaur from North America, *Styracosaurus* measured 18 ft (5.5 m) in length and got its name from the long spikes on its neck frill. Its sharp beak could slice through tough vegetation.

Immensely long wing

Bulbous structure on lower jaw

Trailing foot

AIRBORNE GIANT
Cretaceous pterosaurs included the largest of all flying reptiles. *Ornithocheirus* had a long snout, but its most remarkable feature was its great size. This might have been one of the largest pterosaurs ever—as heavy as a man and with the wingspan of a small plane. *Ornithocheirus* flew above Europe and South America about 125 million years ago.

Wing making downstroke

Beak with small teeth

Sensitive, pointed nose

Lightweight, furry body

Long tail

HERE COME THE BIRDS
The first truly modern birds began to appear in the Cretaceous Period. Hummingbird-sized *Liaoxiornis* was one of the smallest birds from the Mesozoic Era. It lived in eastern Asia early in the Cretaceous Period. *Liaoxiornis* looked like modern birds, but probably belonged to a group of primitive birds called enantiornithes ("opposite birds"). In these birds, a knob on the coracoid bone near the shoulder fit into a basin in the shoulder blade. In birds today, the arrangement is the other way around.

MODERN MAMMALS
New kinds of mammal were emerging in the Cretaceous Period, including *Zalambdalestes*, an early placental mammal, with unborn young nourished by a placenta in the mother's womb. *Zalambdalestes* lived in Late Cretaceous Mongolia and had a long nose like that of an elephant shrew. It hunted in the undergrowth, crushing insects between molar teeth.

SEA MONSTER
At a length of about 40 ft (12.5 m), *Mosasaurus* was one of the largest of the Late Cretaceous marine mosasaur reptiles. The mosasaurs were more closely related to lizards than to dinosaurs. *Mosasaurus* swam with paddle-shaped limbs and a long, flattened tail, seizing fish and ammonites in its huge, sharp-toothed jaws. Its fossils were discovered in 1764 near Maastricht, the Netherlands, and *Mosasaurus* was named after the nearby Meuse River, called *Mosa* in Latin.

SALTASAURUS (75 MYA)
This sauropod was named after the Argentinian province of Salta where its fossils were first found. *Saltasaurus* was 39 ft (12 m) long, with an unusual hide protected by thousands of small, bony lumps.

EDMONTOSAURUS (70 MYA)
Edmontosaurus was one of the last and largest of the hadrosaurs (duck-billed dinosaurs). Up to 43 ft (13 m) long and perhaps as heavy as an elephant, this plant-eater roamed western Canada.

ALBERTOSAURUS (72 MYA)
A predator with a massive head and tiny, two-fingered hands, *Albertosaurus* was somewhat smaller than its close relative *Tyrannosaurus*. Both lived in western North America.

The end of an era

Dinosaurs flourished for more than 160 million years. Then, about 65 million years ago, all disappeared except for the small theropods that we know as birds. Most other sizeable creatures vanished, too, such as the gigantic swimming reptiles and the skin-winged flying reptiles called pterosaurs. Great changes must have happened to the world to drive so many kinds of animal into extinction. At least two great disasters struck. First came a series of massive volcanic eruptions. Then an asteroid (a large lump of rock from space) as big as a city hit Earth with the force of a colossal nuclear explosion.

VOLCANIC ERUPTIONS
Volcanic eruptions in central India at the end of the Cretaceous Period released vast lava flows and huge quantities of dust and toxic gases into the atmosphere. Blown around the world by winds, they could have altered climates in ways that killed many plants and animals.

ASTEROID IMPACT
About 65 million years ago, a molten asteroid 6 miles (10 km) across crashed into Earth at several thousand miles an hour. The fireball struck with the force of more than two million hydrogen bombs, sending enormous shockwaves rippling around the world. Immense clouds of dust hid the Sun for months. The whole planet cooled, which had devastating effects on the world's climate, helping to kill seven out of every ten species of creature that lived on land or at sea.

Fireball striking Earth

Shockwave

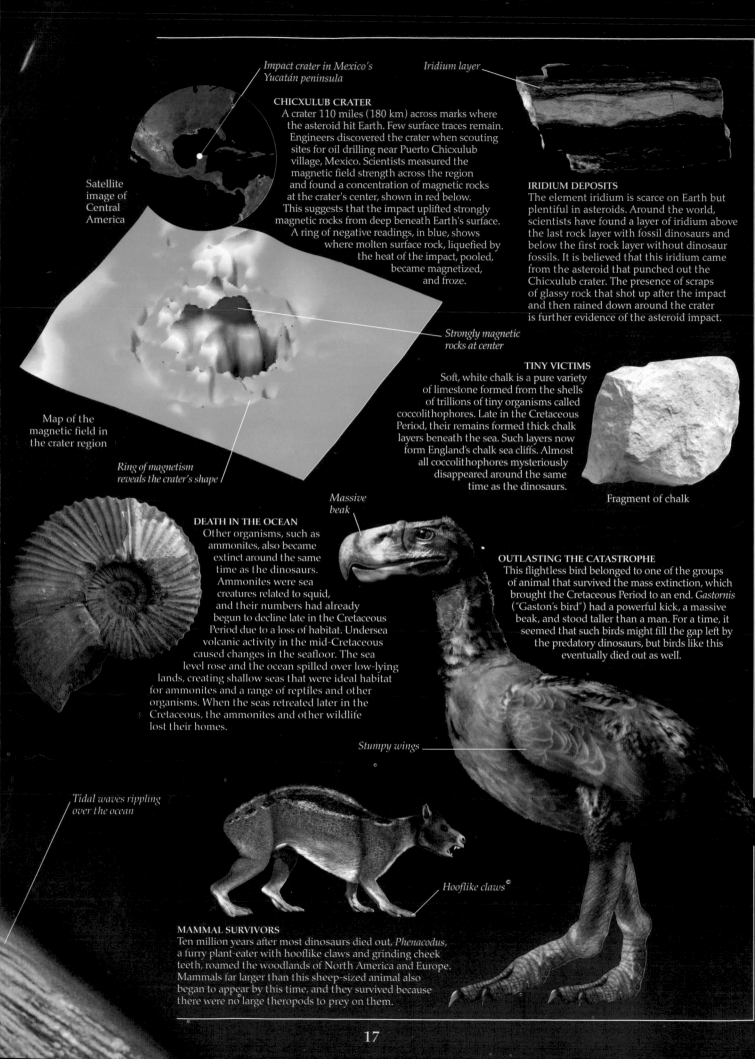

Impact crater in Mexico's
Yucatán peninsula

Iridium layer

CHICXULUB CRATER
A crater 110 miles (180 km) across marks where
the asteroid hit Earth. Few surface traces remain.
Engineers discovered the crater when scouting
sites for oil drilling near Puerto Chicxulub
village, Mexico. Scientists measured the
magnetic field strength across the region
and found a concentration of magnetic rocks
at the crater's center, shown in red below.
This suggests that the impact uplifted strongly
magnetic rocks from deep beneath Earth's surface.
A ring of negative readings, in blue, shows
where molten surface rock, liquefied by
the heat of the impact, pooled,
became magnetized,
and froze.

Satellite
image of
Central
America

IRIDIUM DEPOSITS
The element iridium is scarce on Earth but
plentiful in asteroids. Around the world,
scientists have found a layer of iridium above
the last rock layer with fossil dinosaurs and
below the first rock layer without dinosaur
fossils. It is believed that this iridium came
from the asteroid that punched out the
Chicxulub crater. The presence of scraps
of glassy rock that shot up after the impact
and then rained down around the crater
is further evidence of the asteroid impact.

Strongly magnetic
rocks at center

TINY VICTIMS
Soft, white chalk is a pure variety
of limestone formed from the shells
of trillions of tiny organisms called
coccolithophores. Late in the Cretaceous
Period, their remains formed thick chalk
layers beneath the sea. Such layers now
form England's chalk sea cliffs. Almost
all coccolithophores mysteriously
disappeared around the same
time as the dinosaurs.

Map of the
magnetic field in
the crater region

Ring of magnetism
reveals the crater's shape

Fragment of chalk

Massive
beak

DEATH IN THE OCEAN
Other organisms, such as
ammonites, also became
extinct around the same
time as the dinosaurs.
Ammonites were sea
creatures related to squid,
and their numbers had already
begun to decline late in the Cretaceous
Period due to a loss of habitat. Undersea
volcanic activity in the mid-Cretaceous
caused changes in the seafloor. The sea
level rose and the ocean spilled over low-lying
lands, creating shallow seas that were ideal habitat
for ammonites and a range of reptiles and other
organisms. When the seas retreated later in the
Cretaceous, the ammonites and other wildlife
lost their homes.

OUTLASTING THE CATASTROPHE
This flightless bird belonged to one of the groups
of animal that survived the mass extinction, which
brought the Cretaceous Period to an end. *Gastornis*
("Gaston's bird") had a powerful kick, a massive
beak, and stood taller than a man. For a time, it
seemed that such birds might fill the gap left by
the predatory dinosaurs, but birds like this
eventually died out as well.

Stumpy wings

Tidal waves rippling
over the ocean

Hooflike claws

MAMMAL SURVIVORS
Ten million years after most dinosaurs died out, *Phenacodus*,
a furry plant-eater with hooflike claws and grinding cheek
teeth, roamed the woodlands of North America and Europe.
Mammals far larger than this sheep-sized animal also
began to appear by this time, and they survived because
there were no large theropods to prey on them.

How do we know?

W E KNOW WHAT LONG-DEAD DINOSAURS were like because paleontologists have dug up their remains. Most of these belonged to corpses buried under mud, sand, or volcanic ash that slowly hardened into rock. Minerals filled pores (spaces) in the bones and hardened them, or replaced them altogether, turning bone to stone, in a process called permineralization. All that is left are usually fossilized bones that have been buried in the ground for millions of years. Sometimes, though, the shapes of a body's soft parts—skin, tendons, and muscles—have survived, giving scientists precious, rare glimpses of soft anatomy.

DIGGING UP THE PAST
Paleontologist Luis Chiappe excavates a *Protoceratops* skull at Ukhaa Tolgod in Mongolia's Gobi Desert. Determined dinosaur hunters sometimes travel halfway around the world to reach the best bone beds. There they must often camp and work in harsh conditions and put up with scorching heat or bitter cold.

Dinosaur at riverbank

Bones of recently deceased dinosaurs

Layers building up on top

Stack of layered rocks

Dry riverbed

Dinosaur fossil in rock

ROCK LAYERS
Fossils occur in sedimentary rocks. These are formed when sediment (sand, mud, and gravel) builds up in layers and is compressed over many million years. A series of sedimentary layers can be exposed in a cliff face (as shown here). In an undisturbed set of layers, the oldest rocks lie at the bottom and the youngest at the top. Knowing this, scientists can work out the relative age of each rock layer and the fossils it contains. Index fossils are fossils that are characteristic of a particular period and help to date the rocks in which they are found and also other fossils in neighboring layers of rock. Ammonites, for instance, are index fossils for the Mesozoic Era. Scientists also date rocks accurately by measuring the decay of radioactive elements in them.

THE STORY OF A FOSSIL
From left to right, these block diagrams tell the story of dinosaurs that drowned in a river. Their flesh rotted away, leaving only bones in wet mud when the river dried up. Later, the river refilled, adding more sediment, and buried the bones deeper and deeper in mud that slowly turned into rock. Minerals seeping into pores in the bones changed them into fossils. Over millions of years, wind and rain wore away the rocks, leaving the dinosaur fossils exposed on the surface. There, dinosaur hunters discovered them.

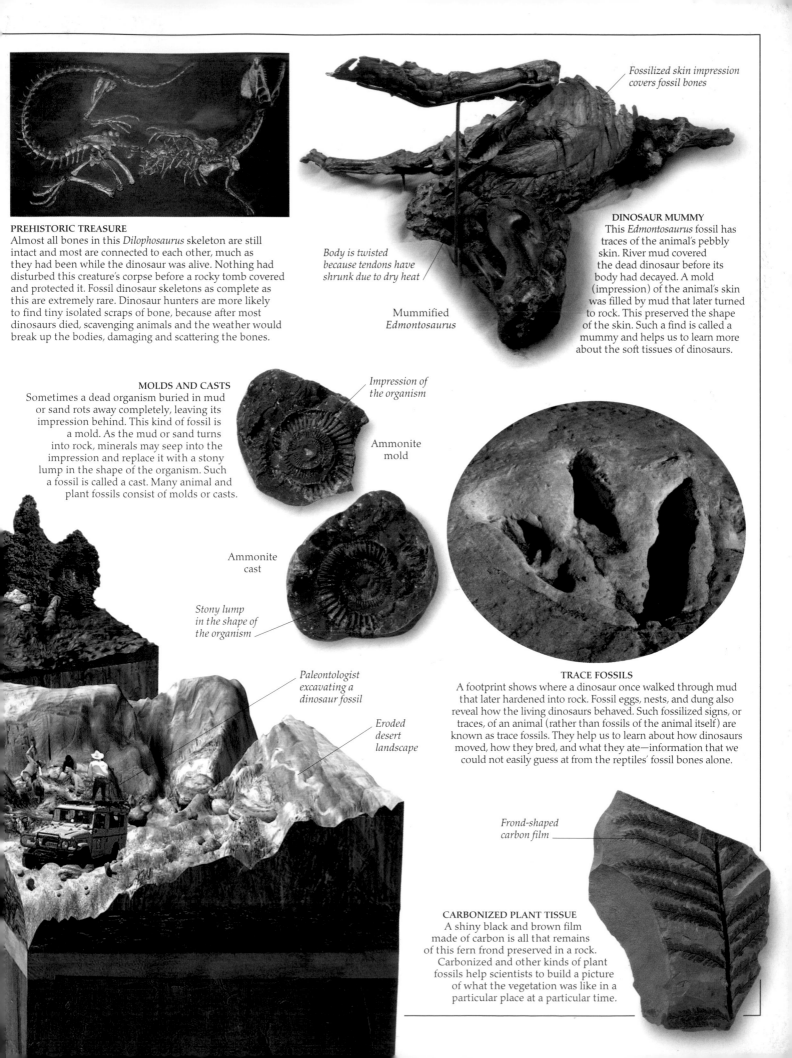

PREHISTORIC TREASURE
Almost all bones in this *Dilophosaurus* skeleton are still intact and most are connected to each other, much as they had been while the dinosaur was alive. Nothing had disturbed this creature's corpse before a rocky tomb covered and protected it. Fossil dinosaur skeletons as complete as this are extremely rare. Dinosaur hunters are more likely to find tiny isolated scraps of bone, because after most dinosaurs died, scavenging animals and the weather would break up the bodies, damaging and scattering the bones.

Fossilized skin impression covers fossil bones

DINOSAUR MUMMY
This *Edmontosaurus* fossil has traces of the animal's pebbly skin. River mud covered the dead dinosaur before its body had decayed. A mold (impression) of the animal's skin was filled by mud that later turned to rock. This preserved the shape of the skin. Such a find is called a mummy and helps us to learn more about the soft tissues of dinosaurs.

Body is twisted because tendons have shrunk due to dry heat

Mummified *Edmontosaurus*

MOLDS AND CASTS
Sometimes a dead organism buried in mud or sand rots away completely, leaving its impression behind. This kind of fossil is a mold. As the mud or sand turns into rock, minerals may seep into the impression and replace it with a stony lump in the shape of the organism. Such a fossil is called a cast. Many animal and plant fossils consist of molds or casts.

Impression of the organism

Ammonite mold

Ammonite cast

Stony lump in the shape of the organism

Paleontologist excavating a dinosaur fossil

Eroded desert landscape

TRACE FOSSILS
A footprint shows where a dinosaur once walked through mud that later hardened into rock. Fossil eggs, nests, and dung also reveal how the living dinosaurs behaved. Such fossilized signs, or traces, of an animal (rather than fossils of the animal itself) are known as trace fossils. They help us to learn about how dinosaurs moved, how they bred, and what they ate—information that we could not easily guess at from the reptiles' fossil bones alone.

Frond-shaped carbon film

CARBONIZED PLANT TISSUE
A shiny black and brown film made of carbon is all that remains of this fern frond preserved in a rock. Carbonized and other kinds of plant fossils help scientists to build a picture of what the vegetation was like in a particular place at a particular time.

The first fossil finds

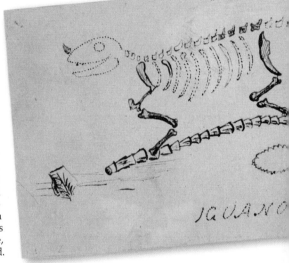

Megalosaurus thigh bone

AN EARLY FIND
This was the first published picture of a dinosaur fossil. In 1677 it featured in a book by Robert Plot, an English museum curator. Plot mistakenly described the fossil as being the thigh bone of a giant man.

PEOPLE HAD BEEN UNEARTHING the fossil bones of giant creatures long before they knew they were discovering what we call dinosaurs. Scientific dinosaur discovery began in England in the early 1820s. A doctor named Gideon Mantell began collecting large fossilized bones and teeth dug up in a Sussex quarry. He believed they came from a giant prehistoric reptile and called it *Iguanodon*. Soon, the bones of two more monstrous animals came to light. The British scientist Richard Owen claimed all three belonged to a single group of reptile, for which he invented the term Dinosauria, meaning "terrible lizards." The term appeared in print for the first time in 1842, and the hunt for dinosaurs would soon spread around the world.

A TOOTHY CLUE
Gideon Mantell (1790–1852) noticed that large fossil teeth like this one resembled the smaller teeth of an iguana lizard. That is why he used the name *Iguanodon*, meaning "iguana toothed." According to one story, Mantell's wife Mary found the first tooth among a pile of stones as she walked along a country lane. In fact, the first find probably came from local quarrymen, who were paid by Mantell to look out for fossil bones.

GUESS AGAIN!
Gideon Mantell drew this sketch to show what he believed *Iguanodon* looked like. No one had yet pieced together a whole dinosaur at this time, so the animal he pictured was largely guesswork based on a few broken bones. The animal resembles an outsized iguana lizard bizarrely perching on a branch. Mantell mistakenly considered a thumb spike to be a horn that jutted from the creature's snout. *Iguanodon*'s tail was also incorrectly shown to be whiplike, instead of being heavy and stiffened.

THE FIRST OF MANY
In 1824, British geologist William Buckland (1784–1856) published his description of *Megalosaurus*'s fossil jaw, similar to one shown here. This dinosaur became the first to get a scientific name. Though Mantell had named *Iguanodon* by 1822, he put its name in print only in 1825. Because scientists officially recognize a specimen when it is published and described, the name *Iguanodon* became the second on a growing list.

Dentary
(bone in lower jaw)

Sharp,
serrated tooth

Megalosaurus jaw

WHAT'S IN A NAME?
Richard Owen (1804–1892) rides the skeleton of a prehistoric giant ground sloth in this cartoon. This anatomist (expert in anatomy) suggested the term "dinosaur" at a time when only three kinds had been discovered. Owen realized that they formed a special group because, unlike ordinary reptiles, they stood on erect limbs and their backbones above the hips were fused together. He published descriptions of many other kinds of prehistoric animal and founded London's Natural History Museum.

LIFESIZE SCULPTURES
The earliest lifesize models of dinosaurs resembled scaly, reptilian rhinoceroses. Installed in 1853, they still stand in Sydenham Park, London. Advised by Richard Owen, sculptor Benjamin Waterhouse Hawkins created concrete models of *Iguanodon*, *Megalosaurus*, and *Hylaeosaurus* and set them up on islands in an artificial lake on public view. Owen led a group of scientists who celebrated the construction by enjoying a lavish banquet inside the hollow body of an *Iguanodon* model.

Concrete *Iguanodon* models

Long front tooth

WILD WILD WEST
Bones of the mini-sauropod *Anchisaurus* had apparently been unearthed in Connecticut as early as 1818. But the spotlight on dinosaur discoveries really shifted from Europe to the American Wild West in the 1870s, when paleontologists began finding fossils of large animals in quarries. The famous American dinosaur hunter Barnum Brown (1873–1963) discovered many fossils in the US. This photograph shows his wife and him examining huge bones found at a quarry in Wyoming in 1941. Brown's earlier finds included the first *Tyrannosaurus* skeleton, dug up in Montana in 1902.

FACT OR FICTION?
The earliest dinosaur discoveries may date back more than 2,600 years. People in central Asia spoke of a creature with a hooked beak and talon-tipped limbs. This mythical monster may have been inspired by a beaked dinosaur called *Protoceratops*, whose fossils have been found in central Asia in recent times. The stories seem to have reached Persia (modern Iran) to the south, where people carved images of the beast. Trade contacts between Persia and Greece may have carried over tales of the legendary creature, giving rise to the Greek legend of the *gryps*, or griffin.

Persian statue of a griffin

Little and large

Sᴀʏ "ᴅɪɴᴏsᴀᴜʀ" ᴀɴᴅ ᴍᴏsᴛ ᴘᴇᴏᴘʟᴇ picture a beast as tall as a house. In fact, most dinosaurs were no bigger than an elephant and weighed less. But some sauropods were the longest and most massive animals ever to walk on land. Built a bit like a giant giraffe, *Brachiosaurus* stood as high as a four-story building. *Diplodocus* measured up to 110 ft (33.5 m)—as long as a row of three buses. Both dinosaurs lived in North America. South America's *Argentinosaurus* was as long as *Diplodocus*, but bulkier— almost as heavy as 10 bull elephants. Perhaps the largest of all dinosaurs was North America's *Amphicoelias*. Sadly, scientists found only part of one of its vertebrae (backbones), then lost it. Any of these giants could have stepped on the tiniest theropods and not even noticed. The theropod *Compsognathus* was little bigger than a chicken. Birdlike *Microraptor* was smaller still. Scientists now know of tinier feathery theropods that are even closer to the origin of birds.

THE HIGH LIFE
A mounted *Barosaurus* skeleton in the American Museum of Natural History gives visitors a notion of the creature's awesome size. If sauropods ever reared, a *Barosaurus* could have towered as high as this mother shown trying to protect her young one from a prowling *Allosaurus*. Her head is 50 ft (15.2 m) above the ground.

EXTREME SIZES
The head-to-tail lengths of these dinosaurs are compared to the height of a human being. Dinosaur giants included the sauropod *Argentinosaurus*. The massive theropod *Carcharodontosaurus* dwarfed *Mei long*, its tiny theropod relation. *Iguanodon* was one of the larger ornithopods and *Triceratops* held the record in terms of size for horned dinosaurs.

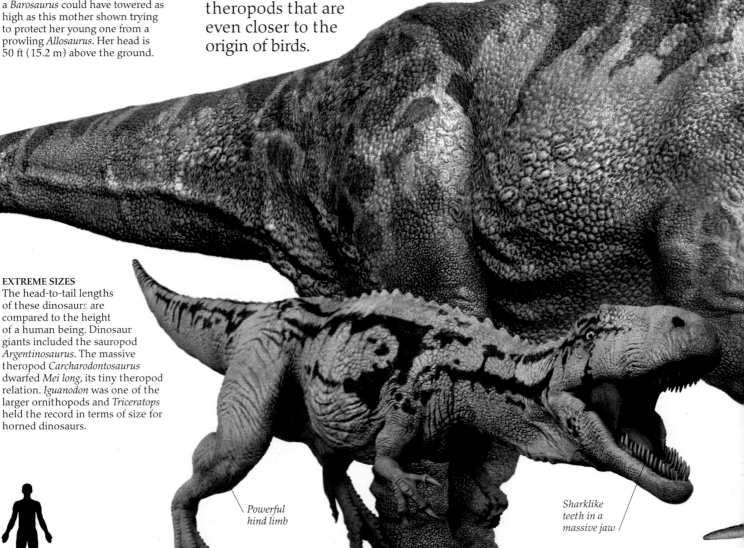

Powerful hind limb

Sharklike teeth in a massive jaw

| Human 6 ft (1.8 m) | *Mei long* 27 in (68.5 cm) | *Carcharodontosaurus* 44 ft (13.5 m) | *Argentinosaurus* 100–110 ft (30.5–33.5 m) |

MOVIE MONSTERS
The huge size of some dinosaurs has inspired a host of monster movies, in which gigantic creatures, such as Godzilla, rampage through modern cities. Scientists know that no dinosaurs ever grew so large, but special visual effects in these popular films have created impossibly large creatures that look very real.

Godzilla terrorizes the streets of New York City

Small head relative to body size

Clawed finger

Feathered legs served as extra wings

DINOSAUR BIPLANE
Microraptor gui was one of the smallest nonbird dinosaurs—bigger than a pigeon, but weighing only 2¼ lb (1 kg). This little theropod measured about 30 in (77 cm) in length and was capable of gliding at least 130 ft (40 m) from tree to tree. *Microraptor zhaoianus*, a related species, was even smaller at 15 in (39 cm) long.

Long neck

Compsognathus

Birdlike foot

Chicken

CHICKEN-SIZED
No bigger than a chicken, *Compsognathus* ("elegant jaw") was once known as the smallest dinosaur. The theropod roamed tropical islands that now form part of southern Germany and France. Scientists discovered that this agile hunter preyed on lizards. They found the remains of a long-tailed lizard called *Bavarisaurus* in the rib cage of a fossil *Compsognathus* specimen.

Head could be lifted to about 16½ ft (5 m) above ground when rearing

Iguanodon
36 ft (11 m)

Triceratops
29½ ft (9 m)

Dinosaur evolution

DINOSAURS SEEM WONDERFULLY WEIRD and different from humans, and yet, their skeletons are based on the same plan as ours. Like us, they had a skull, a backbone, hip bones, and bones to support their arms and legs. The reason for these similarities is that both dinosaurs and humans evolved from the same prehistoric backboned animal. Evolution is the process by which a species gradually changes over time. Certain traits allow some animals to adapt and survive in a changing environment, and, over many generations, these ultimately form a new species. Those that don't adapt die out. For instance, from a fish with fins evolved four-legged animals that bred in water, and eventually on land. One group of these animals became our mammal ancestors. Another group evolved into reptiles, and from sprawling reptiles came the dinosaurs.

FISHY FORERUNNER
Panderichthys was a fish that lived about 380 million years ago. An animal like this was the ancestor of all tetrapods (four-legged, backboned animals). The pectoral fins on its sides and pelvic fins on the underside of its body sprouted from fleshy lobes (stalked structures) that were strengthened by bones like those found in our limbs. Its skull bones, ribs, and the enamel covering its teeth were more like those of tetrapods than fish.

THE FIRST CREATURES WITH LEGS
Acanthostega was one of the earliest tetrapods and one of the first vertebrates (backboned animals) with recognizable limbs. It lived in shallow water around 360 million years ago and had features found in fish as well as those of tetrapods. Like fish, *Acanthostega* had gills and a tail fin. It had no true elbows, wrists, knees, or ankles. But like most tetrapods, it had hip bones, limb bones, toes, and fingers. Unlike fish, its spine was stiffened by interlocking vertebrae (backbones), and its head moved separately from its shoulders.

Paddlelike tail fin

Acanthostega

Eight digits

ANCESTORS OF REPTILES
Westlothiana might have been one of the first four-legged animals to live and breed on land. Early tetrapods laid eggs in water, and the eggs dried up when they were out of the water. Then some began producing eggs protected by a membrane called an amnion. This group of animals, known as amniotes, were the ancestors of reptiles and mammals. *Westlothiana* lived 330 million years ago and may have been an early amniote.

Westlothiana

Five digits

Lizardlike tail

Sprawling leg

Euparkeria

Leg tucked in

Chasmatosaurus

A SPRAWLING WALKER
Crocodile-like *Chasmatosaurus* belonged to a group of reptiles called archosaurs ("ruling reptiles"). This group also included crocodiles and dinosaurs. With limbs that stuck out sideways, *Chasmatosaurus* walked in the sprawling way that lizards do. It lived about 250 million years ago.

REARING TO RUN
Agile archosaurs such as cat-sized *Euparkeria* were the descendants of the early, sprawling kinds. *Euparkeria* lived about 245 million years ago. It walked on all fours, but this reptile's hind limbs were longer than its forelimbs and fairly well tucked in beneath its body. It probably reared to run on its hind limbs only, balanced by its long tail.

Pelvis
(hip bone)

Dorsal vertebra
(backbone)

Skull

Caudal vertebra
(tail bone)

Rib

Manus
(hand)

Tibia
(shin bone)

Phalanx
(toe bone)

Tyrannosaurus
skeleton

Skull

Vertebra

Manus
(hand)

Coccyx
(tail bone)

Rib

Pelvis
(hip bone)

Phalanx
(toe bone)

Tibia
(shin bone)

Human
skeleton

SKELETONS COMPARED
Strip off their skin and flesh, and you can
match the skeletons of this *Tyrannosaurus*
and human being almost bone for bone.
Their bones bear the same names, because
they both inherited them from the same
fishy ancestor. The main difference between
the pictured skeletons is in the number and
proportion of some bones. *Tyrannosaurus*
has a longer skull, although the human
skull is also large in proportion to the
body. The dinosaur has enough vertebrae
to form a long tail, while humans have
one tail bone, known as the coccyx.

DINOSAUR DAWN
One of the earliest dinosaurs was *Eoraptor*
("dawn thief"), which lived 228 million years
ago. Like all theropods, this small, two-legged
hunter had erect legs and grasping hands for
seizing prey. But it lacked some features seen in
most saurischians (lizard-hipped dinosaurs).
For instance, its neck and thumbs were
relatively shorter than those of other
theropods or sauropodomorphs.

Eoraptor

Heads and brains

A DINOSAUR'S HEAD was built around a skull made up of separate bones that slotted together to support the jaws and protect the brain. There were holes for eyes, ears, nostrils, and jaw muscles, and often extra holes that saved weight. Dinosaur heads came in a variety of shapes and sizes. Some skulls were lightly built, with slender bones. Other dinosaurs had heavy, solid-looking armored skulls. Each skull enclosed a brain that was relatively smaller and less complex than the brains of most mammals. Some theropods had brains as large as those in certain modern birds. These dinosaurs may have had very keen senses and could probably respond swiftly to their surroundings.

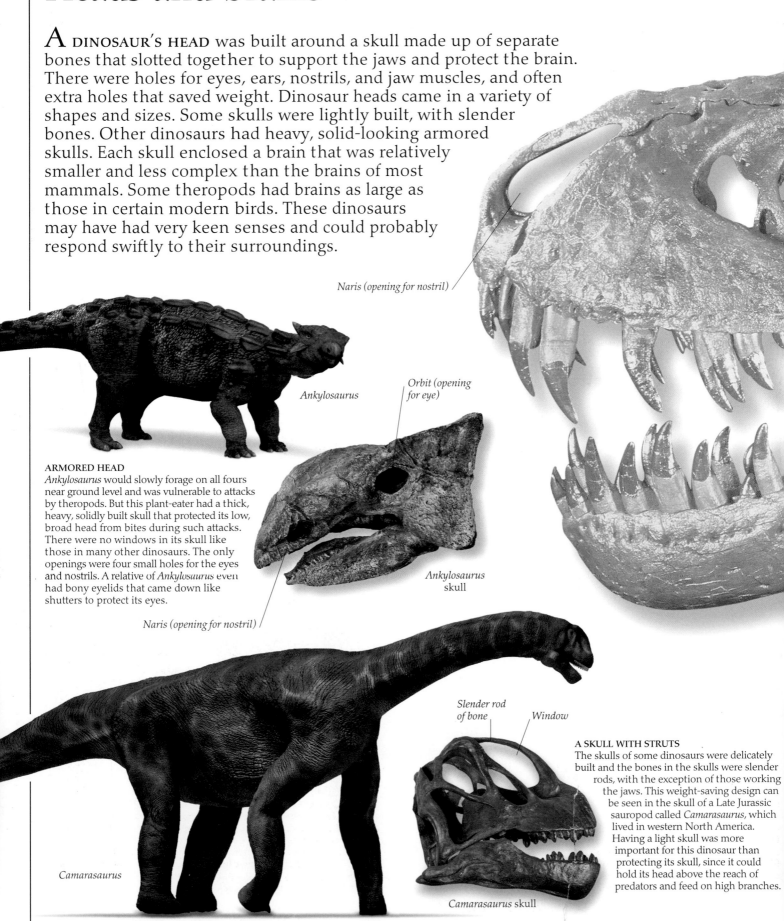

Naris (opening for nostril)

Ankylosaurus

Orbit (opening for eye)

ARMORED HEAD
Ankylosaurus would slowly forage on all fours near ground level and was vulnerable to attacks by theropods. But this plant-eater had a thick, heavy, solidly built skull that protected its low, broad head from bites during such attacks. There were no windows in its skull like those in many other dinosaurs. The only openings were four small holes for the eyes and nostrils. A relative of *Ankylosaurus* even had bony eyelids that came down like shutters to protect its eyes.

Ankylosaurus skull

Naris (opening for nostril)

Camarasaurus

Slender rod of bone

Window

A SKULL WITH STRUTS
The skulls of some dinosaurs were delicately built and the bones in the skulls were slender rods, with the exception of those working the jaws. This weight-saving design can be seen in the skull of a Late Jurassic sauropod called *Camarasaurus*, which lived in western North America. Having a light skull was more important for this dinosaur than protecting its skull, since it could hold its head above the reach of predators and feed on high branches.

Camarasaurus skull

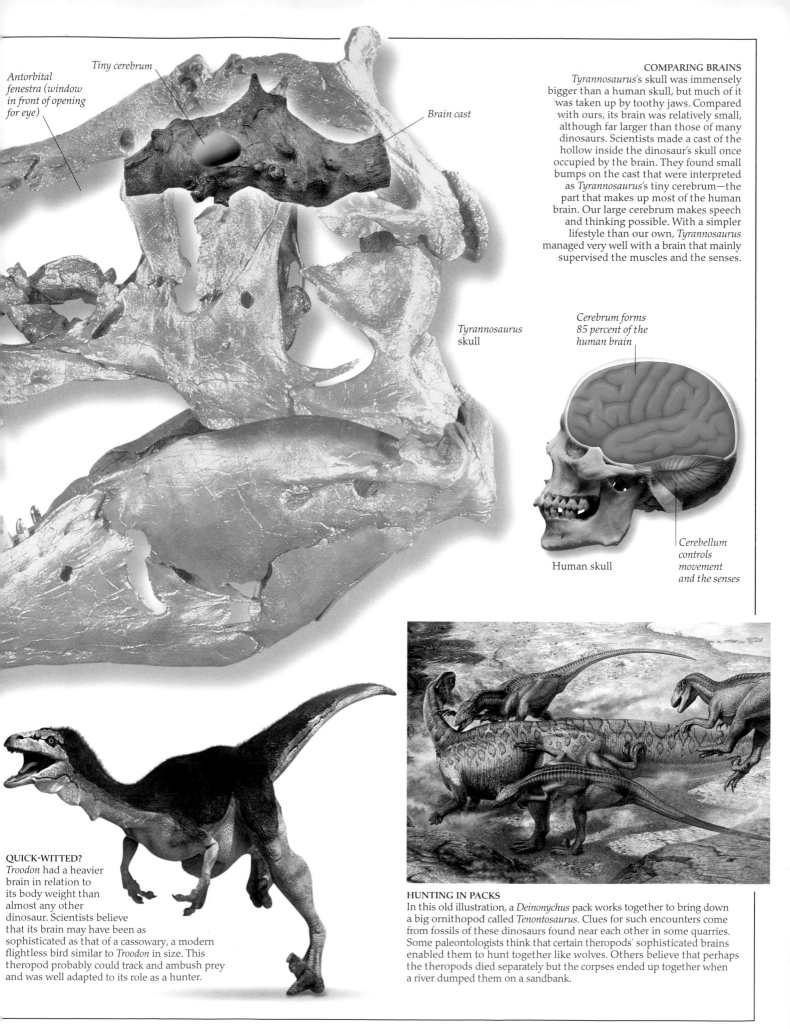

Antorbital
fenestra (window
in front of opening
for eye)

Tiny cerebrum

Brain cast

COMPARING BRAINS
Tyrannosaurus's skull was immensely
bigger than a human skull, but much of it
was taken up by toothy jaws. Compared
with ours, its brain was relatively small,
although far larger than those of many
dinosaurs. Scientists made a cast of the
hollow inside the dinosaur's skull once
occupied by the brain. They found small
bumps on the cast that were interpreted
as *Tyrannosaurus*'s tiny cerebrum—the
part that makes up most of the human
brain. Our large cerebrum makes speech
and thinking possible. With a simpler
lifestyle than our own, *Tyrannosaurus*
managed very well with a brain that mainly
supervised the muscles and the senses.

Tyrannosaurus
skull

Cerebrum forms
85 percent of the
human brain

Cerebellum
controls
movement
and the senses

Human skull

QUICK-WITTED?
Troodon had a heavier
brain in relation to
its body weight than
almost any other
dinosaur. Scientists believe
that its brain may have been as
sophisticated as that of a cassowary, a modern
flightless bird similar to *Troodon* in size. This
theropod probably could track and ambush prey
and was well adapted to its role as a hunter.

HUNTING IN PACKS
In this old illustration, a *Deinonychus* pack works together to bring down
a big ornithopod called *Tenontosaurus*. Clues for such encounters come
from fossils of these dinosaurs found near each other in some quarries.
Some paleontologists think that certain theropods' sophisticated brains
enabled them to hunt together like wolves. Others believe that perhaps
the theropods died separately but the corpses ended up together when
a river dumped them on a sandbank.

Horns and head crests

THE SKULLS OF MANY DINOSAURS had bumps, horns, or head crests. The dinosaurs probably used these either for display—to scare a rival or impress a mate—or to act as signals that helped other dinosaurs to spot fellow members of their species from a distance. Head crests that were made of thin, fragile bone would have been used only for display. But skulls with sturdy bumps and horns could have served as weapons of attack or defense. Thickened skulls seemed to have been made for butting heads with rivals, and long horns for jabbing, or shoving, if the horns of two rivals were to interlock. But perhaps the most effective use of bumps, crests, and horns was to frighten off enemies or predators.

THREE-HORNED FACE
Two brow horns 3½ ft (1 m) long and a short nose horn earned *Triceratops* its name, which means "three-horned face." Males probably flaunted horns at one another threateningly and sometimes had actual clashes. The bony shield at the back of the head saved their necks from injury. Fossil skulls show signs of bone that regrew after damage.

Long brow horn

Small nose horn

A THICK NOSE
Instead of the sharp nose horn of most large plant-eating ceratopsians, *Pachyrhinosaurus* ("thick-nosed lizard") grew a bony lump that was broad and flattish. The lump developed as a thick mass of spongy outgrowth from bones that roofed the nose. The lumps in some individuals dipped in the middle, while those in others bulged. Perhaps males grew one kind and females the other. Rival males very likely met bump to bump and pushed until the weaker male gave way. Like other ceratopsians, *Pachyrhinosaurus* lived in the western part of North America late in the Cretaceous Period.

Helmet-shaped skull roof

Narrow beak

THICK-HEADED
Pachycephalosaurs ("thick-headed lizards") such as *Stegoceras* had immensely thick skull roofs. These might have functioned as crash helmets to protect the brains when rival males bashed heads together. Or perhaps males dominated their rivals by brandishing their domes in a display of threat. Many animals today use horns or fangs in this way, instead of risking injury by fighting.

READY TO FIGHT
Every fall, rival male deer size each other up, parading their antlers in an openly threatening posture. If two stags seem evenly matched, both will lock antlers and try to shove each other backward. The winner earns the right to mate with many females. Jousting in this way, large deer with dangerous headgear show how some horned dinosaurs might have behaved.

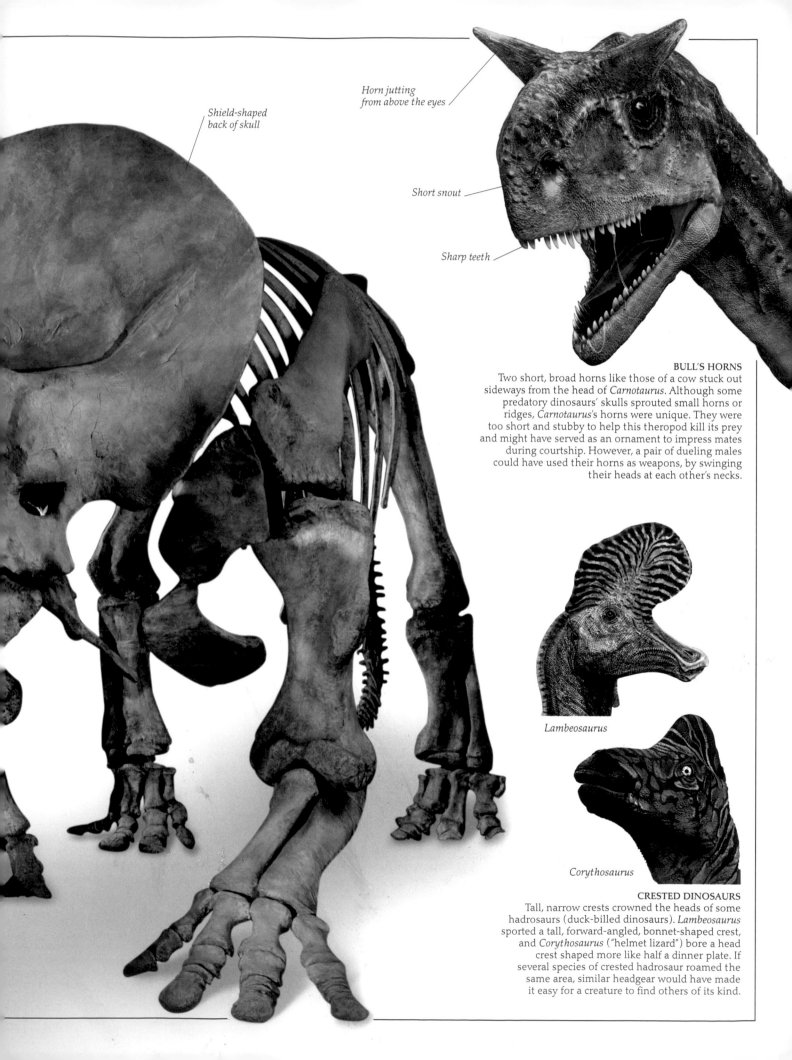

*Shield-shaped
back of skull*

*Horn jutting
from above the eyes*

Short snout

Sharp teeth

BULL'S HORNS
Two short, broad horns like those of a cow stuck out sideways from the head of *Carnotaurus*. Although some predatory dinosaurs' skulls sprouted small horns or ridges, *Carnotaurus*'s horns were unique. They were too short and stubby to help this theropod kill its prey and might have served as an ornament to impress mates during courtship. However, a pair of dueling males could have used their horns as weapons, by swinging their heads at each other's necks.

Lambeosaurus

Corythosaurus

CRESTED DINOSAURS
Tall, narrow crests crowned the heads of some hadrosaurs (duck-billed dinosaurs). *Lambeosaurus* sported a tall, forward-angled, bonnet-shaped crest, and *Corythosaurus* ("helmet lizard") bore a head crest shaped more like half a dinner plate. If several species of crested hadrosaur roamed the same area, similar headgear would have made it easy for a creature to find others of its kind.

Senses and communication

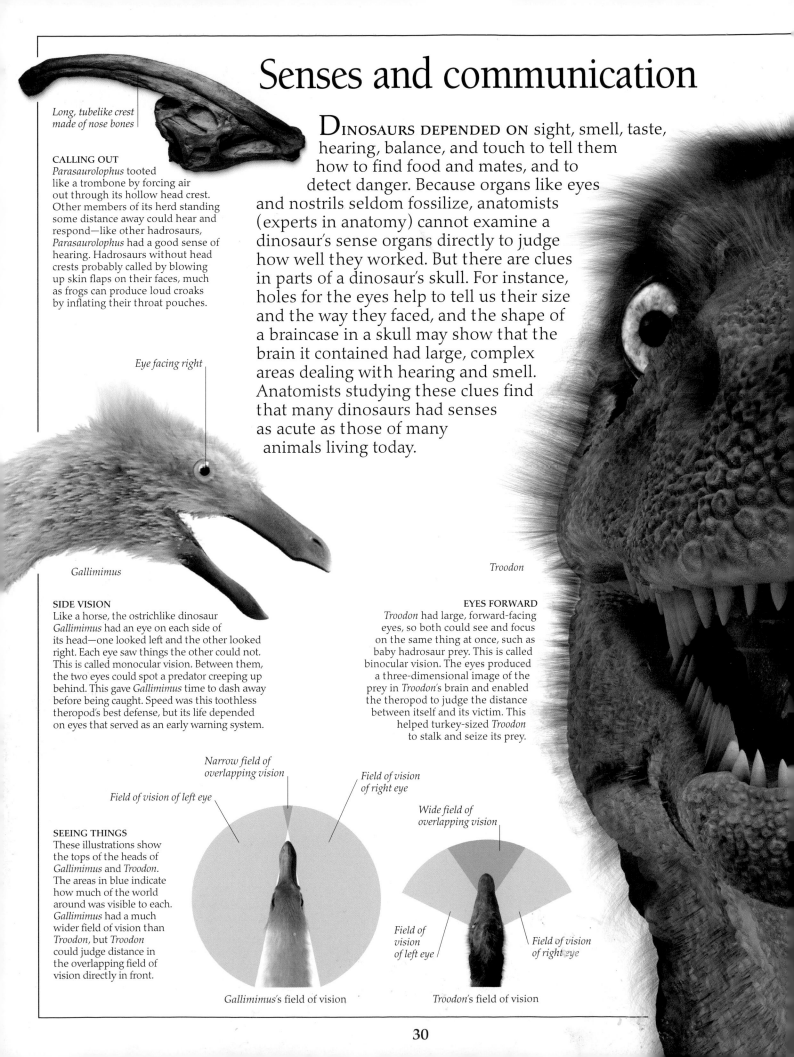

Long, tubelike crest made of nose bones

CALLING OUT
Parasaurolophus tooted like a trombone by forcing air out through its hollow head crest. Other members of its herd standing some distance away could hear and respond—like other hadrosaurs, *Parasaurolophus* had a good sense of hearing. Hadrosaurs without head crests probably called by blowing up skin flaps on their faces, much as frogs can produce loud croaks by inflating their throat pouches.

DINOSAURS DEPENDED ON sight, smell, taste, hearing, balance, and touch to tell them how to find food and mates, and to detect danger. Because organs like eyes and nostrils seldom fossilize, anatomists (experts in anatomy) cannot examine a dinosaur's sense organs directly to judge how well they worked. But there are clues in parts of a dinosaur's skull. For instance, holes for the eyes help to tell us their size and the way they faced, and the shape of a braincase in a skull may show that the brain it contained had large, complex areas dealing with hearing and smell. Anatomists studying these clues find that many dinosaurs had senses as acute as those of many animals living today.

Eye facing right

Gallimimus

Troodon

SIDE VISION
Like a horse, the ostrichlike dinosaur *Gallimimus* had an eye on each side of its head—one looked left and the other looked right. Each eye saw things the other could not. This is called monocular vision. Between them, the two eyes could spot a predator creeping up behind. This gave *Gallimimus* time to dash away before being caught. Speed was this toothless theropod's best defense, but its life depended on eyes that served as an early warning system.

EYES FORWARD
Troodon had large, forward-facing eyes, so both could see and focus on the same thing at once, such as baby hadrosaur prey. This is called binocular vision. The eyes produced a three-dimensional image of the prey in *Troodon's* brain and enabled the theropod to judge the distance between itself and its victim. This helped turkey-sized *Troodon* to stalk and seize its prey.

Narrow field of overlapping vision

Field of vision of left eye

Field of vision of right eye

Wide field of overlapping vision

SEEING THINGS
These illustrations show the tops of the heads of *Gallimimus* and *Troodon*. The areas in blue indicate how much of the world around was visible to each. *Gallimimus* had a much wider field of vision than *Troodon*, but *Troodon* could judge distance in the overlapping field of vision directly in front.

Field of vision of left eye

Field of vision of right eye

Gallimimus's field of vision

Troodon's field of vision

Large eye with good nocturnal (night) vision

Eye facing forward

IN THE DARK
Leaellynasaura was a small ornithopod with large eyes and big optic lobes—parts of the brain that interpret what the eyes see. Scientists believe this means that *Leaellynasaura* could see well in the dark, which helped this small plant-eater to live through a long winter night lasting for weeks. *Leaellynasaura* lived in southern Australia about 110 million years ago—a time when that part of the world lay close to Earth's south pole and was therefore covered in darkness in winter.

SNIFFING IT OUT
Tyrannosaurus ("tyrant lizard") had large olfactory lobes—parts of the brain that interpret what the nose smells. This suggests that this Late Cretaceous theropod possessed a keen sense of smell. Like a turkey vulture, it could probably scent a dead body lying around half a mile (1 km) away. Some people believe that *Tyrannosaurus* ate only dead dinosaurs. This meat-eater might have scavenged some of its food, but *Tyrannosaurus* was probably a hunter-killer as well.

Head crest

BRIGHT AND COLORFUL
Bright colors might have adorned the head crest of *Cryolophosaurus* ("frozen crested lizard"), a large theropod found in an icy Antarctic mountain. Colorful skin, crests, or feathers could have helped male theropods to attract mates. This would have worked only if these dinosaurs could tell different colors apart. We can be pretty sure that they could, however, because birds can identify colors and birds are theropods, too.

HIDING IN PLAIN SIGHT
Standing among tree ferns, a greenish *Iguanodon* would have been almost invisible to its predators. No one knows what this animal's skin color really was, but many dinosaurs were probably colored or patterned with spots or stripes so that they matched their surroundings. Just as with some living wild mammals, color camouflage would have helped plant-eaters to avoid being eaten, and hunters to creep up on their prey.

31

Meat-eaters

Many large meat-eating dinosaurs had jaws used as weapons for killing and tearing up big game. The head was large, with strong muscles powering jaws that were rimmed with knifelike teeth. These were used to cut through the skin and flesh of bulky plant-eating dinosaurs with ease. *Allosaurus* would use its powerful jaws to seize and kill its victim, then tear off massive chunks of meat. But not all theropods had heads for tackling such heavy tasks. The heads of spinosaurids were shaped for seizing fish. Small, sharp-toothed coelurosaurs swallowed lizards whole. Beaked ornithomimids ("ostrich mimics") were toothless and snapped up insects, but also fed on leaves and fruit.

Serrated edge

Cracks due to fossilization

New tooth

KILLING TEETH
With serrated edges like a steak knife, the curved teeth of *Megalosaurus* sliced easily through flesh. They were even strong enough to crunch through bone. Such hard use made them wear out fairly fast, and some even snapped off. But new teeth always grew to replace those worn out or lost.

Large, curved tooth of Megalosaurus

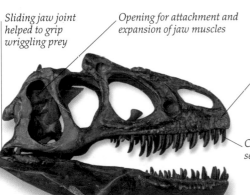

Sliding jaw joint helped to grip wriggling prey

Opening for attachment and expansion of jaw muscles

Maxilla (upper jaw)

Curved, serrated tooth

Mandible (lower jaw)

Tarbosaurus

Barsboldia

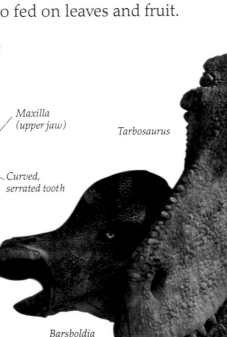

TOP CHOPPER
The sturdiest bones in an *Allosaurus*'s skull supported jaw muscles and bladelike teeth. *Allosaurus* would snap its jaws shut on a victim, then slice off flesh with its sharp teeth. The skull was specialized for rapid chopping rather than forceful biting, and this theropod probably could not crush bones in the same way as *Tyrannosaurus*.

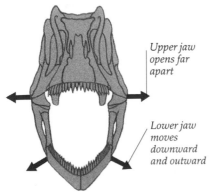

Upper jaw opens far apart

Lower jaw moves downward and outward

OPEN WIDE
Allosaurus's skull was loosely constructed and there were movable joints between some of the bones. This meant that the jaws could not only gape wide apart, but could also expand outward to engulf huge chunks of meat.

TYRANNOSAUR ATTACK
This *Tarbosaurus* ("terrible lizard") has clamped its powerful jaws on the neck of a young *Barsboldia*—a hadrosaur named after Mongolian paleontologist Rinchen Barsbold. Both dinosaurs lived in the eastern part of central Asia, late in the Cretaceous Period. *Tarbosaurus* grew nearly as huge as its American cousin *Tyrannosaurus*, and, like its relative, probably preyed on hadrosaur herds. Too slow to catch big or fit animals, *Tarbosaurus* preyed on the sick, old, and young. It attacked by tearing off mouthfuls of flesh and bone with great lunging bites. It also scavenged on dead animals.

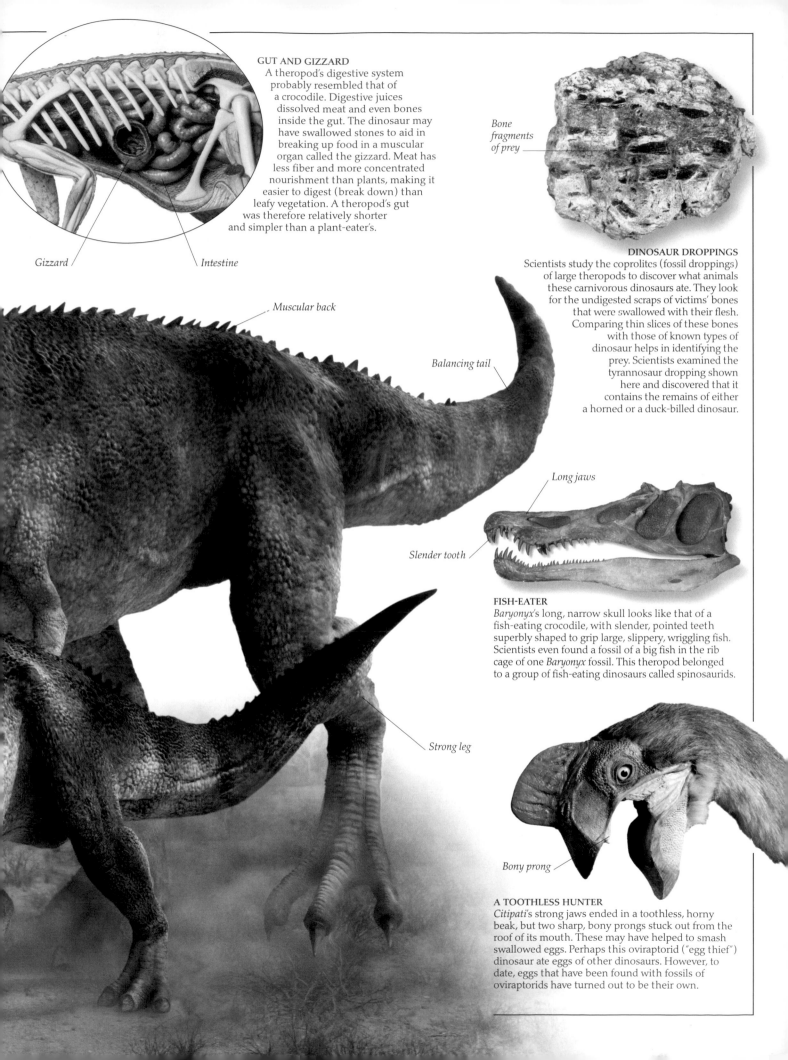

GUT AND GIZZARD
A theropod's digestive system probably resembled that of a crocodile. Digestive juices dissolved meat and even bones inside the gut. The dinosaur may have swallowed stones to aid in breaking up food in a muscular organ called the gizzard. Meat has less fiber and more concentrated nourishment than plants, making it easier to digest (break down) than leafy vegetation. A theropod's gut was therefore relatively shorter and simpler than a plant-eater's.

Gizzard

Intestine

Bone fragments of prey

DINOSAUR DROPPINGS
Scientists study the coprolites (fossil droppings) of large theropods to discover what animals these carnivorous dinosaurs ate. They look for the undigested scraps of victims' bones that were swallowed with their flesh. Comparing thin slices of these bones with those of known types of dinosaur helps in identifying the prey. Scientists examined the tyrannosaur dropping shown here and discovered that it contains the remains of either a horned or a duck-billed dinosaur.

Muscular back

Balancing tail

Long jaws

Slender tooth

FISH-EATER
Baryonyx's long, narrow skull looks like that of a fish-eating crocodile, with slender, pointed teeth superbly shaped to grip large, slippery, wriggling fish. Scientists even found a fossil of a big fish in the rib cage of one *Baryonyx* fossil. This theropod belonged to a group of fish-eating dinosaurs called spinosaurids.

Strong leg

Bony prong

A TOOTHLESS HUNTER
Citipati's strong jaws ended in a toothless, horny beak, but two sharp, bony prongs stuck out from the roof of its mouth. These may have helped to smash swallowed eggs. Perhaps this oviraptorid ("egg thief") dinosaur ate eggs of other dinosaurs. However, to date, eggs that have been found with fossils of oviraptorids have turned out to be their own.

Plant-eaters

THE JAWS, TEETH, STOMACH, AND GUT of herbivorous (plant-eating) dinosaurs were made for cropping, chewing, and digesting vegetation. Broad-snouted armored dinosaurs were unfussy eaters, while armored dinosaurs with a narrow snout picked out just the plants they liked. Sauropods stripped twigs with teeth shaped like spoons or pencils, then swallowed leafy mouthfuls whole. The beaks of horned dinosaurs sliced through tough, fibrous vegetation that their sharp cheek teeth chewed into pulp. Hadrosaurs (duck-billed dinosaurs) cropped leaves with their toothless beaks and chewed them with batteries of cheek teeth. Most ornithischians probably had fleshy cheeks to hold food while chewing. All of these herbivores had long intestines to digest large amounts of plant food.

Square jaw

Numerous teeth

MOWING MACHINE
Nigersaurus had more teeth than any other sauropod, and these lined the front of its shovel-shaped mouth. Its lower jaw alone bore 68 teeth, and behind each pencil-shaped front tooth grew many more to replace the teeth as they wore out one by one. *Nigersaurus* was short-necked and could not graze on foliage high up in the trees. Like a living lawnmower, it cropped low-growing ferns and horsetails.

Small intestine

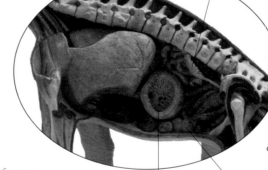

SAUROPOD DIGESTIVE SYSTEM
Leaves swallowed by a sauropod passed through its long intestine, where they were digested into simple substances that could be absorbed into the blood and carried around the body. Leaves are not very nourishing, so sauropods had to eat lots to fuel their large bodies. The ancestors of sauropods walked on their hind limbs, but the weight of the guts held in front of the hip bones caused them to evolve (become adapted) over time to walking on all fours.

Large intestine

Gizzard

STONES IN THE GUT
Smooth stones found in the remains of some sauropods led paleontologists to believe that the dinosaurs swallowed them for use as millstones. Sauropods may have had a gizzard (muscular organ for grinding food) like a bird's. Gastroliths ("stomach stones") were thought to have ground up plant matter in the gizzard. But German scientists found that stones in the gizzards of ostriches were rough. They concluded that the sauropods swallowed stones either by accident, or deliberately for the nourishing minerals in the stones.

Sharp edge of new tooth helped in shredding leaves

Tooth worn down by eating plants

WEAR AND TEAR
Two saw-edged *Iguanodon* cheek teeth—one new, the other worn—show the effects of chewing tough plants such as horsetails rich in the abrasive substance silica. Each time *Iguanodon* bit off a leafy mouthful and closed its mouth, the two side rows of upper teeth slid across the surface of the lower teeth, grinding the leaves. This kept the teeth sharp, but also wore them down.

Iguanodon teeth

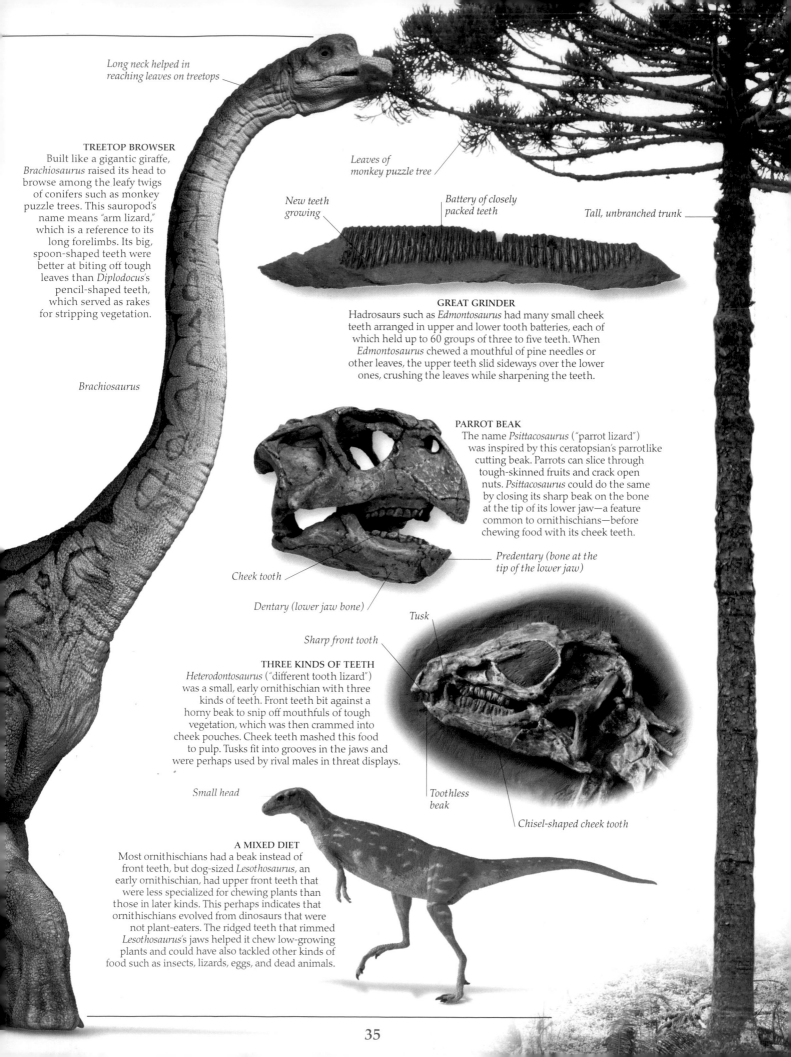

TREETOP BROWSER
Built like a gigantic giraffe, *Brachiosaurus* raised its head to browse among the leafy twigs of conifers such as monkey puzzle trees. This sauropod's name means "arm lizard," which is a reference to its long forelimbs. Its big, spoon-shaped teeth were better at biting off tough leaves than *Diplodocus*'s pencil-shaped teeth, which served as rakes for stripping vegetation.

Long neck helped in reaching leaves on treetops

Brachiosaurus

Leaves of monkey puzzle tree

New teeth growing

Battery of closely packed teeth

Tall, unbranched trunk

GREAT GRINDER
Hadrosaurs such as *Edmontosaurus* had many small cheek teeth arranged in upper and lower tooth batteries, each of which held up to 60 groups of three to five teeth. When *Edmontosaurus* chewed a mouthful of pine needles or other leaves, the upper teeth slid sideways over the lower ones, crushing the leaves while sharpening the teeth.

PARROT BEAK
The name *Psittacosaurus* ("parrot lizard") was inspired by this ceratopsian's parrotlike cutting beak. Parrots can slice through tough-skinned fruits and crack open nuts. *Psittacosaurus* could do the same by closing its sharp beak on the bone at the tip of its lower jaw—a feature common to ornithischians—before chewing food with its cheek teeth.

Predentary (bone at the tip of the lower jaw)

Cheek tooth

Dentary (lower jaw bone)

Tusk

Sharp front tooth

THREE KINDS OF TEETH
Heterodontosaurus ("different tooth lizard") was a small, early ornithischian with three kinds of teeth. Front teeth bit against a horny beak to snip off mouthfuls of tough vegetation, which was then crammed into cheek pouches. Cheek teeth mashed this food to pulp. Tusks fit into grooves in the jaws and were perhaps used by rival males in threat displays.

Toothless beak

Chisel-shaped cheek tooth

Small head

A MIXED DIET
Most ornithischians had a beak instead of front teeth, but dog-sized *Lesothosaurus*, an early ornithischian, had upper front teeth that were less specialized for chewing plants than those in later kinds. This perhaps indicates that ornithischians evolved from dinosaurs that were not plant-eaters. The ridged teeth that rimmed *Lesothosaurus*'s jaws helped it chew low-growing plants and could have also tackled other kinds of food such as insects, lizards, eggs, and dead animals.

Long and short necks

SAUROPODS HAD THE LONGEST NECKS of all dinosaurs—some more than five times as long as a giraffe's. Prosauropods and sauropods were the first animals that could graze on treetop leaves while standing on the ground. In contrast, most armored, plated, and horned dinosaurs had short, strong necks, and generally fed on vegetation near the ground. The length of a plant-eating dinosaur's neck determined which levels of vegetation it could browse. Theropods had a muscular S-shaped neck, like a bird's. Large meat-eaters, such as *Tyrannosaurus*, had massive necks, while smaller theropods, such as *Velociraptor*, had slim necks that uncoiled like springs when attacking prey.

Cervical vertebra (neck bone)

Mandible (lower jaw)

Muscles running along the topside of the neck raised the head

BRACED FOR HEADY HEIGHTS
Powerful neck muscles lifted *Brachiosaurus*'s head and a strong heart pumped blood up to its brain. This sauropod's neck was supported at the base in the same way that the movable jib (projecting arm) of a crane is supported by a tower and base. Raising the heavy load of the head and neck would have been difficult for *Brachiosaurus* due to the effects of gravity. This is why all sauropod necks needed bracing, which came from the muscles, tendons, and the cablelike ligament above the neck bones. Maybe bracing was also helped by ribs that grew back from each neck bone to overlap the bone behind. Bracing strengthened sauropod necks so that they could function as flexible rods.

Crane with movable jib

Head lifted to about 42 ft (13 m) above ground

JURASSIC GIANTS
A *Brachiosaurus* herd would have wandered through riverside forests of conifers, cycads, and ferns. The great sauropods lowered their necks to drink and lifted them to feed. The herds would feed first on leaves growing lower down and then graze through foliage at the treetops. To reach that height, these gigantic creatures might have had to raise their heads to the height of a four-story office building.

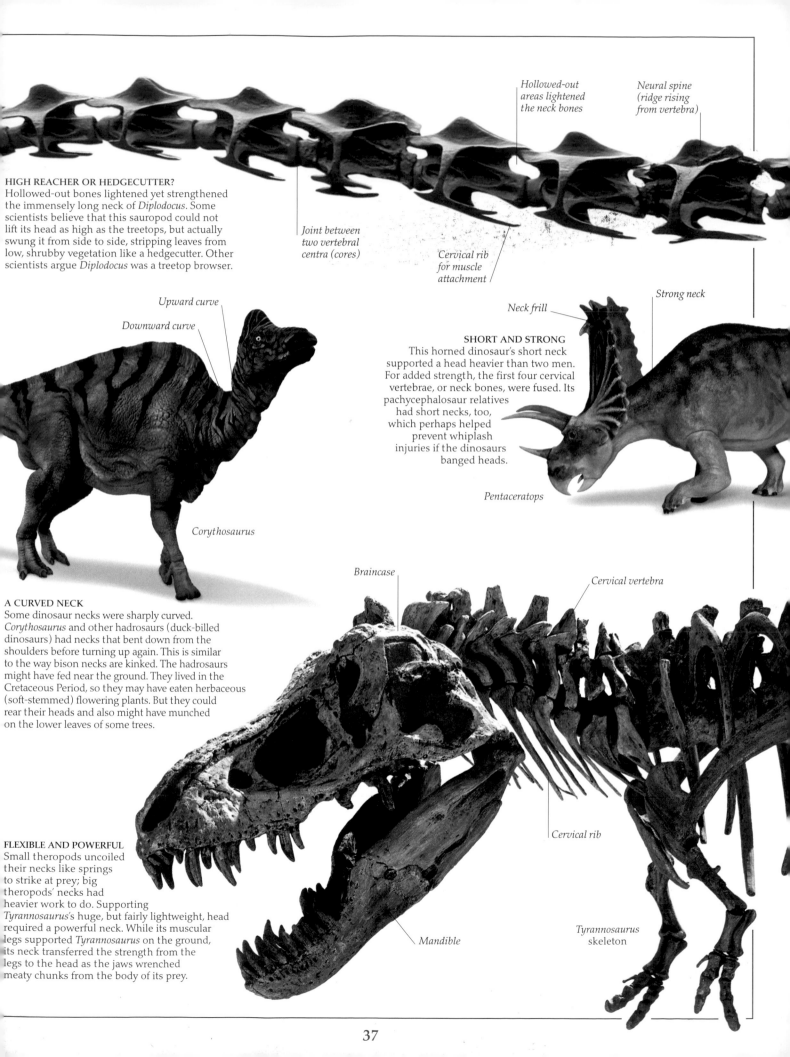

Hollowed-out areas lightened the neck bones

Neural spine (ridge rising from vertebra)

HIGH REACHER OR HEDGECUTTER?
Hollowed-out bones lightened yet strengthened the immensely long neck of *Diplodocus*. Some scientists believe that this sauropod could not lift its head as high as the treetops, but actually swung it from side to side, stripping leaves from low, shrubby vegetation like a hedgecutter. Other scientists argue *Diplodocus* was a treetop browser.

Joint between two vertebral centra (cores)

Cervical rib for muscle attachment

Upward curve

Downward curve

Neck frill

Strong neck

SHORT AND STRONG
This horned dinosaur's short neck supported a head heavier than two men. For added strength, the first four cervical vertebrae, or neck bones, were fused. Its pachycephalosaur relatives had short necks, too, which perhaps helped prevent whiplash injuries if the dinosaurs banged heads.

Pentaceratops

Corythosaurus

A CURVED NECK
Some dinosaur necks were sharply curved. *Corythosaurus* and other hadrosaurs (duck-billed dinosaurs) had necks that bent down from the shoulders before turning up again. This is similar to the way bison necks are kinked. The hadrosaurs might have fed near the ground. They lived in the Cretaceous Period, so they may have eaten herbaceous (soft-stemmed) flowering plants. But they could rear their heads and also might have munched on the lower leaves of some trees.

Braincase

Cervical vertebra

Cervical rib

Tyrannosaurus skeleton

FLEXIBLE AND POWERFUL
Small theropods uncoiled their necks like springs to strike at prey; big theropods' necks had heavier work to do. Supporting *Tyrannosaurus*'s huge, but fairly lightweight, head required a powerful neck. While its muscular legs supported *Tyrannosaurus* on the ground, its neck transferred the strength from the legs to the head as the jaws wrenched meaty chunks from the body of its prey.

Mandible

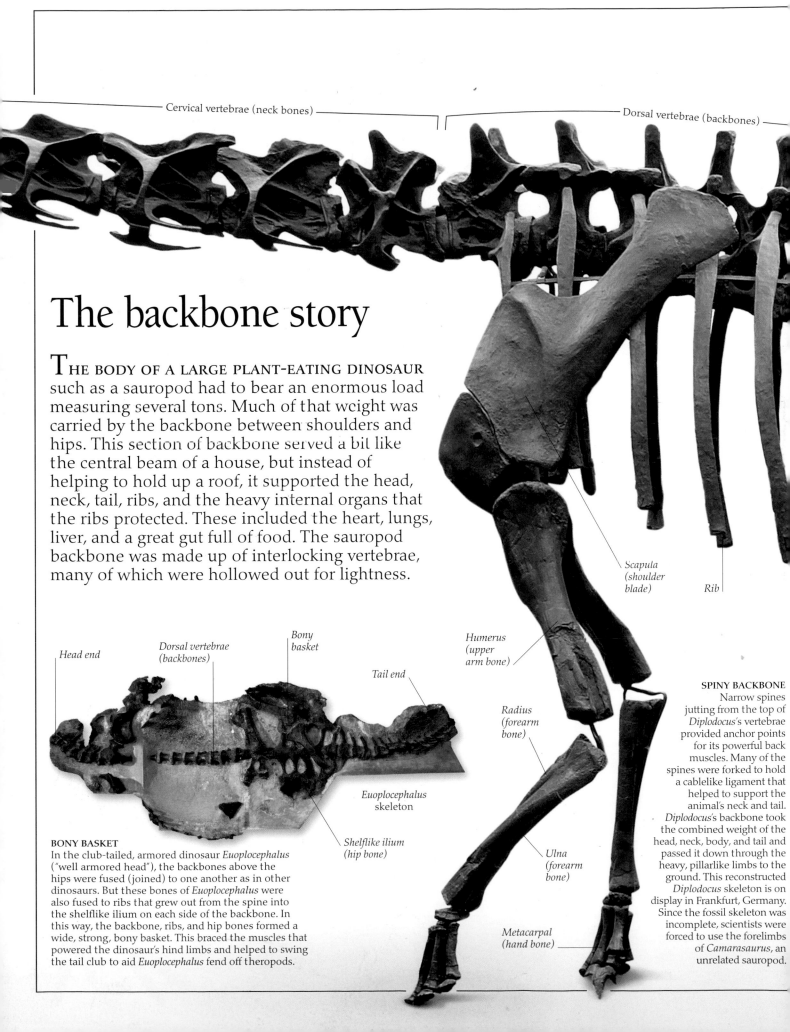

Cervical vertebrae (neck bones)

Dorsal vertebrae (backbones)

The backbone story

THE BODY OF A LARGE PLANT-EATING DINOSAUR such as a sauropod had to bear an enormous load measuring several tons. Much of that weight was carried by the backbone between shoulders and hips. This section of backbone served a bit like the central beam of a house, but instead of helping to hold up a roof, it supported the head, neck, tail, ribs, and the heavy internal organs that the ribs protected. These included the heart, lungs, liver, and a great gut full of food. The sauropod backbone was made up of interlocking vertebrae, many of which were hollowed out for lightness.

Scapula (shoulder blade)

Rib

Head end

Dorsal vertebrae (backbones)

Bony basket

Tail end

Humerus (upper arm bone)

Radius (forearm bone)

Euoplocephalus skeleton

Shelflike ilium (hip bone)

Ulna (forearm bone)

Metacarpal (hand bone)

BONY BASKET
In the club-tailed, armored dinosaur *Euoplocephalus* ("well armored head"), the backbones above the hips were fused (joined) to one another as in other dinosaurs. But these bones of *Euoplocephalus* were also fused to ribs that grew out from the spine into the shelflike ilium on each side of the backbone. In this way, the backbone, ribs, and hip bones formed a wide, strong, bony basket. This braced the muscles that powered the dinosaur's hind limbs and helped to swing the tail club to aid *Euoplocephalus* fend off theropods.

SPINY BACKBONE
Narrow spines jutting from the top of *Diplodocus*'s vertebrae provided anchor points for its powerful back muscles. Many of the spines were forked to hold a cablelike ligament that helped to support the animal's neck and tail. *Diplodocus*'s backbone took the combined weight of the head, neck, body, and tail and passed it down through the heavy, pillarlike limbs to the ground. This reconstructed *Diplodocus* skeleton is on display in Frankfurt, Germany. Since the fossil skeleton was incomplete, scientists were forced to use the forelimbs of *Camarasaurus*, an unrelated sauropod.

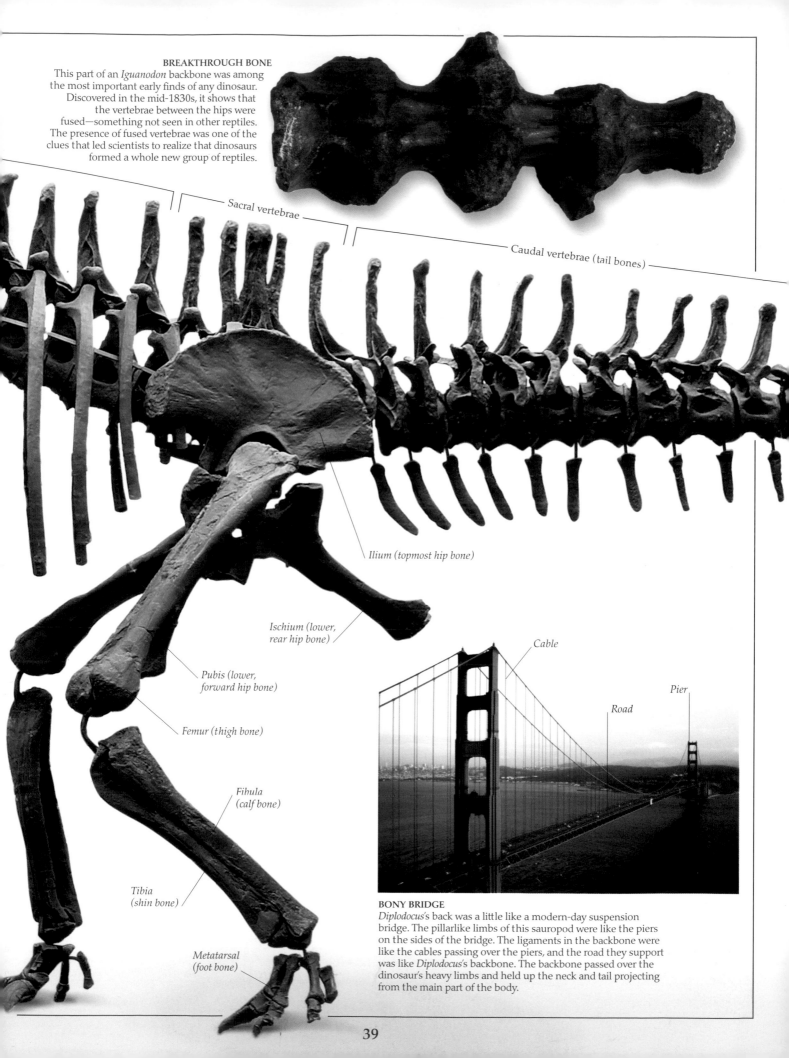

BREAKTHROUGH BONE
This part of an *Iguanodon* backbone was among the most important early finds of any dinosaur. Discovered in the mid-1830s, it shows that the vertebrae between the hips were fused—something not seen in other reptiles. The presence of fused vertebrae was one of the clues that led scientists to realize that dinosaurs formed a whole new group of reptiles.

Sacral vertebrae

Caudal vertebrae (tail bones)

Ilium (topmost hip bone)

Ischium (lower, rear hip bone)

Cable

Road

Pier

Pubis (lower, forward hip bone)

Femur (thigh bone)

Fibula (calf bone)

Tibia (shin bone)

Metatarsal (foot bone)

BONY BRIDGE
Diplodocus's back was a little like a modern-day suspension bridge. The pillarlike limbs of this sauropod were like the piers on the sides of the bridge. The ligaments in the backbone were like the cables passing over the piers, and the road they support was like *Diplodocus's* backbone. The backbone passed over the dinosaur's heavy limbs and held up the neck and tail projecting from the main part of the body.

All about tails

DINOSAURS USED THEIR TAILS for many different purposes. Most importantly, the tails helped the animals to move around. Each side of a dinosaur's tail anchored a muscle that pulled the leg on that side backward in order to push the body forward. Because a muscle pulls at both ends at once, most theropods' tails must have waggled from side to side as they walked. Tails also helped front-heavy dinosaurs to keep their balance as they walked or ran. And a sauropod rearing its head might have supported its body on a tripod made up of its tail and both hind limbs.

RODLIKE TAIL
Deinonychus swished its tail from side to side to keep its balance as it chased and leapt upon its prey. This feathered theropod's long tail stuck out like a ramrod thanks to stiffening structures on the tail that locked together all the tail bones except those closest to the dinosaur's body. Such a tail was typical of the dromaeosaurids—the group of birdlike theropods that *Deinonychus* belonged to.

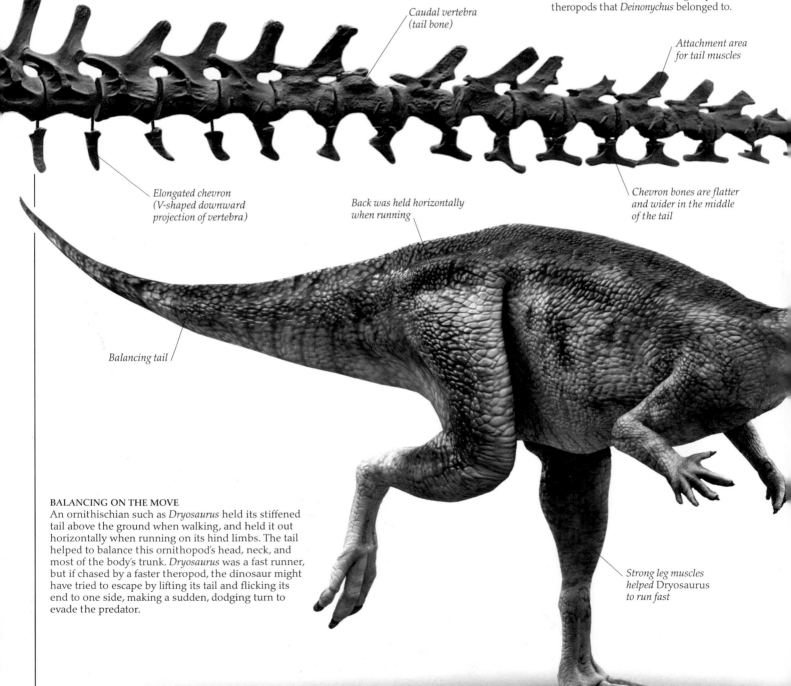

Caudal vertebra (tail bone)

Attachment area for tail muscles

Elongated chevron (V-shaped downward projection of vertebra)

Back was held horizontally when running

Chevron bones are flatter and wider in the middle of the tail

Balancing tail

BALANCING ON THE MOVE
An ornithischian such as *Dryosaurus* held its stiffened tail above the ground when walking, and held it out horizontally when running on its hind limbs. The tail helped to balance this ornithopod's head, neck, and most of the body's trunk. *Dryosaurus* was a fast runner, but if chased by a faster theropod, the dinosaur might have tried to escape by lifting its tail and flicking its end to one side, making a sudden, dodging turn to evade the predator.

Strong leg muscles helped Dryosaurus to run fast

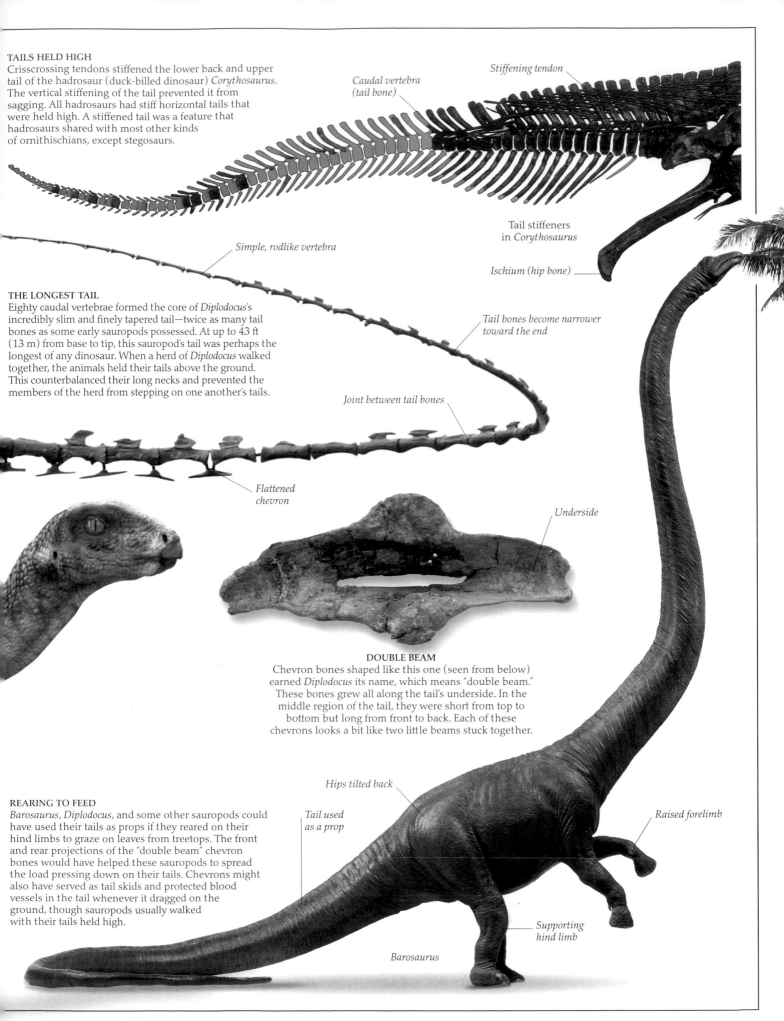

TAILS HELD HIGH

Crisscrossing tendons stiffened the lower back and upper tail of the hadrosaur (duck-billed dinosaur) *Corythosaurus*. The vertical stiffening of the tail prevented it from sagging. All hadrosaurs had stiff horizontal tails that were held high. A stiffened tail was a feature that hadrosaurs shared with most other kinds of ornithischians, except stegosaurs.

Stiffening tendon

Caudal vertebra (tail bone)

Tail stiffeners in *Corythosaurus*

Ischium (hip bone)

Simple, rodlike vertebra

THE LONGEST TAIL

Eighty caudal vertebrae formed the core of *Diplodocus*'s incredibly slim and finely tapered tail—twice as many tail bones as some early sauropods possessed. At up to 43 ft (13 m) from base to tip, this sauropod's tail was perhaps the longest of any dinosaur. When a herd of *Diplodocus* walked together, the animals held their tails above the ground. This counterbalanced their long necks and prevented the members of the herd from stepping on one another's tails.

Tail bones become narrower toward the end

Joint between tail bones

Flattened chevron

Underside

DOUBLE BEAM

Chevron bones shaped like this one (seen from below) earned *Diplodocus* its name, which means "double beam." These bones grew all along the tail's underside. In the middle region of the tail, they were short from top to bottom but long from front to back. Each of these chevrons looks a bit like two little beams stuck together.

Hips tilted back

Raised forelimb

REARING TO FEED

Barosaurus, Diplodocus, and some other sauropods could have used their tails as props if they reared on their hind limbs to graze on leaves from treetops. The front and rear projections of the "double beam" chevron bones would have helped these sauropods to spread the load pressing down on their tails. Chevrons might also have served as tail skids and protected blood vessels in the tail whenever it dragged on the ground, though sauropods usually walked with their tails held high.

Tail used as a prop

Supporting hind limb

Barosaurus

41

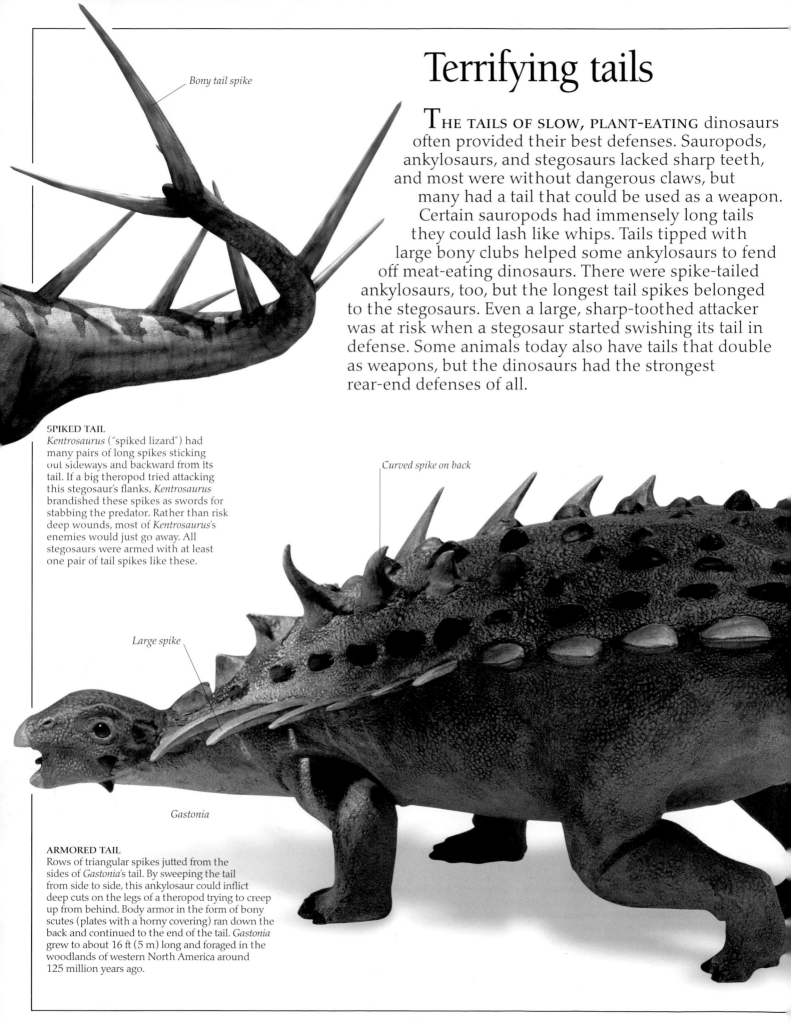

Bony tail spike

Terrifying tails

THE TAILS OF SLOW, PLANT-EATING dinosaurs often provided their best defenses. Sauropods, ankylosaurs, and stegosaurs lacked sharp teeth, and most were without dangerous claws, but many had a tail that could be used as a weapon. Certain sauropods had immensely long tails they could lash like whips. Tails tipped with large bony clubs helped some ankylosaurs to fend off meat-eating dinosaurs. There were spike-tailed ankylosaurs, too, but the longest tail spikes belonged to the stegosaurs. Even a large, sharp-toothed attacker was at risk when a stegosaur started swishing its tail in defense. Some animals today also have tails that double as weapons, but the dinosaurs had the strongest rear-end defenses of all.

SPIKED TAIL
Kentrosaurus ("spiked lizard") had many pairs of long spikes sticking out sideways and backward from its tail. If a big theropod tried attacking this stegosaur's flanks, Kentrosaurus brandished these spikes as swords for stabbing the predator. Rather than risk deep wounds, most of Kentrosaurus's enemies would just go away. All stegosaurs were armed with at least one pair of tail spikes like these.

Curved spike on back

Large spike

Gastonia

ARMORED TAIL
Rows of triangular spikes jutted from the sides of Gastonia's tail. By sweeping the tail from side to side, this ankylosaur could inflict deep cuts on the legs of a theropod trying to creep up from behind. Body armor in the form of bony scutes (plates with a horny covering) ran down the back and continued to the end of the tail. Gastonia grew to about 16 ft (5 m) long and foraged in the woodlands of western North America around 125 million years ago.

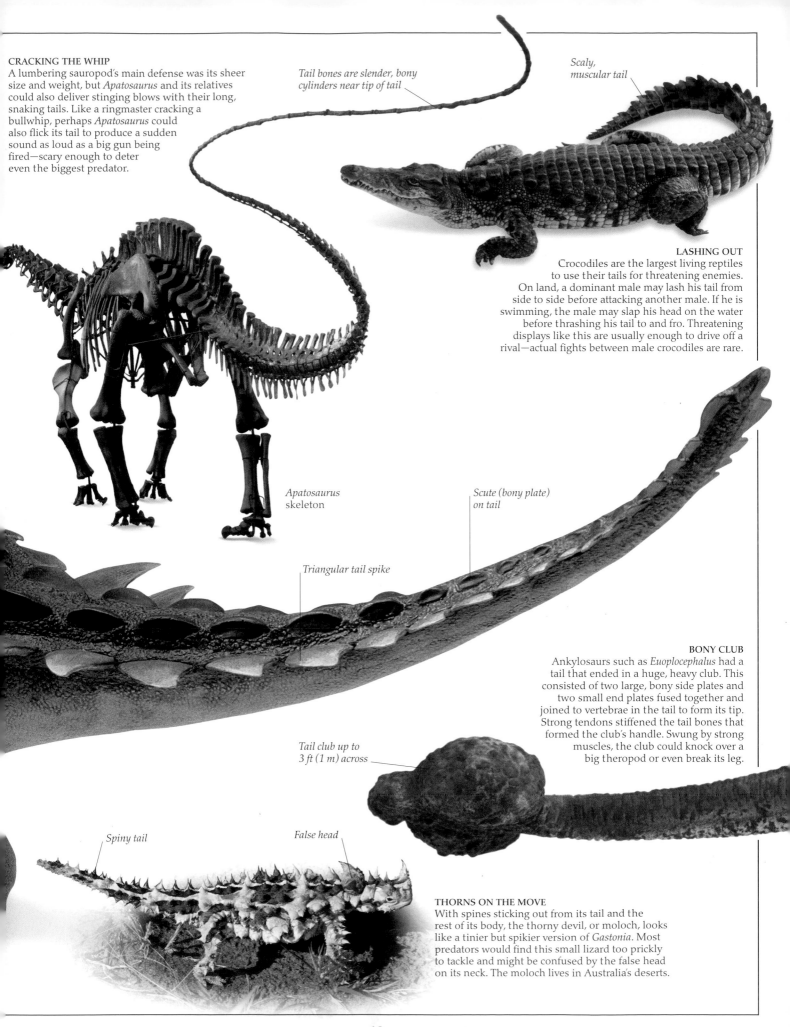

CRACKING THE WHIP
A lumbering sauropod's main defense was its sheer size and weight, but *Apatosaurus* and its relatives could also deliver stinging blows with their long, snaking tails. Like a ringmaster cracking a bullwhip, perhaps *Apatosaurus* could also flick its tail to produce a sudden sound as loud as a big gun being fired—scary enough to deter even the biggest predator.

Tail bones are slender, bony cylinders near tip of tail

Scaly, muscular tail

LASHING OUT
Crocodiles are the largest living reptiles to use their tails for threatening enemies. On land, a dominant male may lash his tail from side to side before attacking another male. If he is swimming, the male may slap his head on the water before thrashing his tail to and fro. Threatening displays like this are usually enough to drive off a rival—actual fights between male crocodiles are rare.

Apatosaurus skeleton

Scute (bony plate) on tail

Triangular tail spike

BONY CLUB
Ankylosaurs such as *Euoplocephalus* had a tail that ended in a huge, heavy club. This consisted of two large, bony side plates and two small end plates fused together and joined to vertebrae in the tail to form its tip. Strong tendons stiffened the tail bones that formed the club's handle. Swung by strong muscles, the club could knock over a big theropod or even break its leg.

Tail club up to 3 ft (1 m) across

Spiny tail

False head

THORNS ON THE MOVE
With spines sticking out from its tail and the rest of its body, the thorny devil, or moloch, looks like a tinier but spikier version of *Gastonia*. Most predators would find this small lizard too prickly to tackle and might be confused by the false head on its neck. The moloch lives in Australia's deserts.

Plates and sails

IN THE LATE JURASSIC WOODLANDS, massive *Stegosaurus* with its distinctive rows of plates on its back must have been quite a sight! Features such as plates, sails, and humps ran down the backs of many other dinosaurs. We know this from rows of tall bony spines, blades, and slabs found on the fossil backbones of these animals. Strange arrays of these structures were present in stegosaurs and some unusual sauropods, ornithopods, and theropods. They were covered with either horny sheaths, skin, or fatty tissue. But scientists still argue about the exact purpose of these structures.

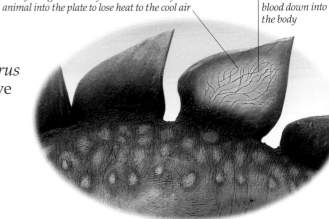

Artery brings hot blood from the interior of the overheated animal into the plate to lose heat to the cool air

Vein takes cooled blood down into the body

HEATED DEBATE
Some scientists believe that *Stegosaurus*'s plates may have been covered in skin. The blood vessels below the skin would adjust the body temperature by absorbing heat if the plates faced the Sun, and shedding heat if not. But others believe that the plates were covered in dead tissue like horn, which contains no blood vessels, and so the plates couldn't have functioned as heat exchangers.

Sail or ridge

Slender snout

SAIL BACK
Spinosaurus ("spine lizard") was an immense theropod with a long snout and may have fed on fish as well as other dinosaurs. Neural spines (spiny pieces of bone rising from the vertebrae) up to 6 ft (1.8 m) long jutted from its backbone like sword blades. These spines formed a bony scaffolding that held up a skin sail or fatty ridge. *Spinosaurus* perhaps used it as an eye-catching display to attract mates, as a food store for body fat, as a radiator to cool its body, or as a heat shield.

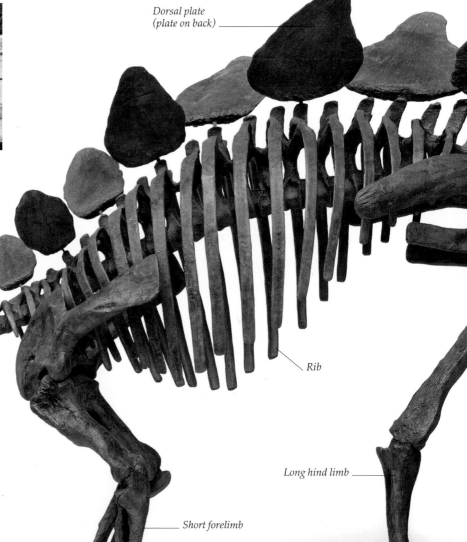

Dorsal plate (plate on back)

Rib

Long hind limb

Short forelimb

Cervical plate (neck plate)

Small skull

PLATED DINOSAUR
Stegosaurus ("roof lizard") was the largest of all the plated dinosaurs, or stegosaurs. These were four-legged ornithischians with a tiny head and toothless beak. Most kinds of stegosaur sported a double row of tall spikes, but alternating plates ridged *Stegosaurus*'s neck, back, and tail. These spikes and plates helped members of different species of stegosaur to recognize others of their own kind. *Stegosaurus* was about 30 ft (9 m) long, and the plates made it look even bigger, probably forcing even larger theropods to think twice before attacking it.

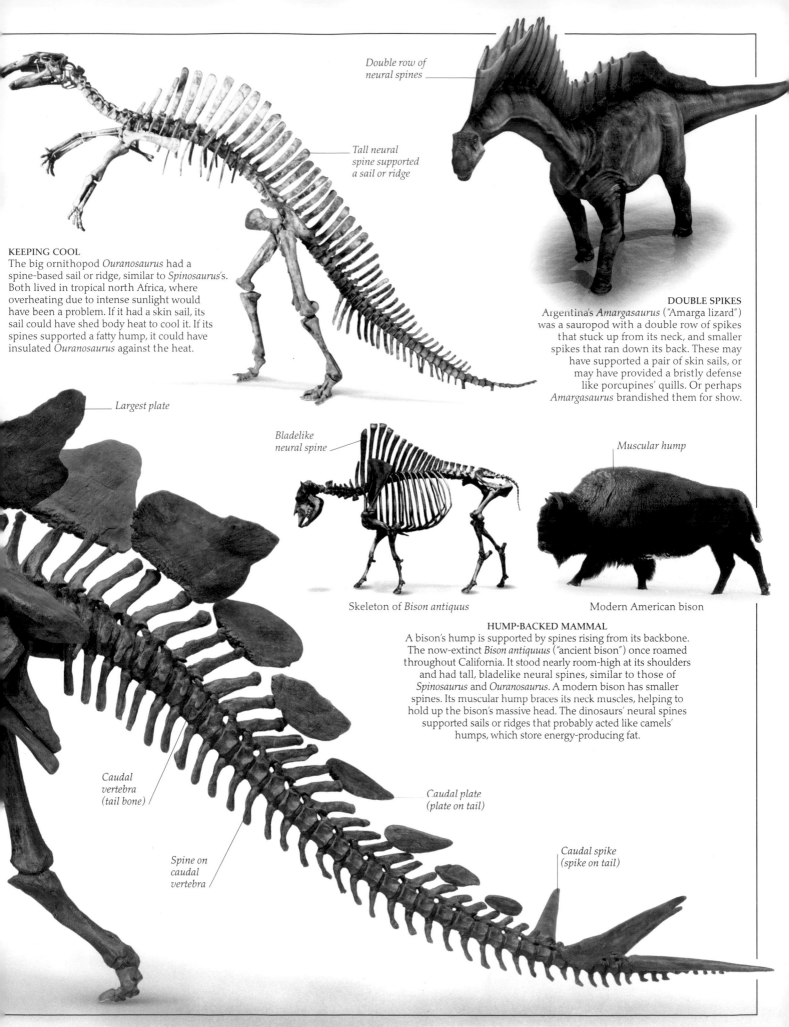

Double row of neural spines

Tall neural spine supported a sail or ridge

KEEPING COOL

The big ornithopod *Ouranosaurus* had a spine-based sail or ridge, similar to *Spinosaurus*'s. Both lived in tropical north Africa, where overheating due to intense sunlight would have been a problem. If it had a skin sail, its sail could have shed body heat to cool it. If its spines supported a fatty hump, it could have insulated *Ouranosaurus* against the heat.

DOUBLE SPIKES

Argentina's *Amargasaurus* ("Amarga lizard") was a sauropod with a double row of spikes that stuck up from its neck, and smaller spikes that ran down its back. These may have supported a pair of skin sails, or may have provided a bristly defense like porcupines' quills. Or perhaps *Amargasaurus* brandished them for show.

Largest plate

Bladelike neural spine

Muscular hump

Skeleton of *Bison antiquus*

Modern American bison

HUMP-BACKED MAMMAL

A bison's hump is supported by spines rising from its backbone. The now-extinct *Bison antiquuus* ("ancient bison") once roamed throughout California. It stood nearly room-high at its shoulders and had tall, bladelike neural spines, similar to those of *Spinosaurus* and *Ouranosaurus*. A modern bison has smaller spines. Its muscular hump braces its neck muscles, helping to hold up the bison's massive head. The dinosaurs' neural spines supported sails or ridges that probably acted like camels' humps, which store energy-producing fat.

Caudal vertebra (tail bone)

Spine on caudal vertebra

Caudal plate (plate on tail)

Caudal spike (spike on tail)

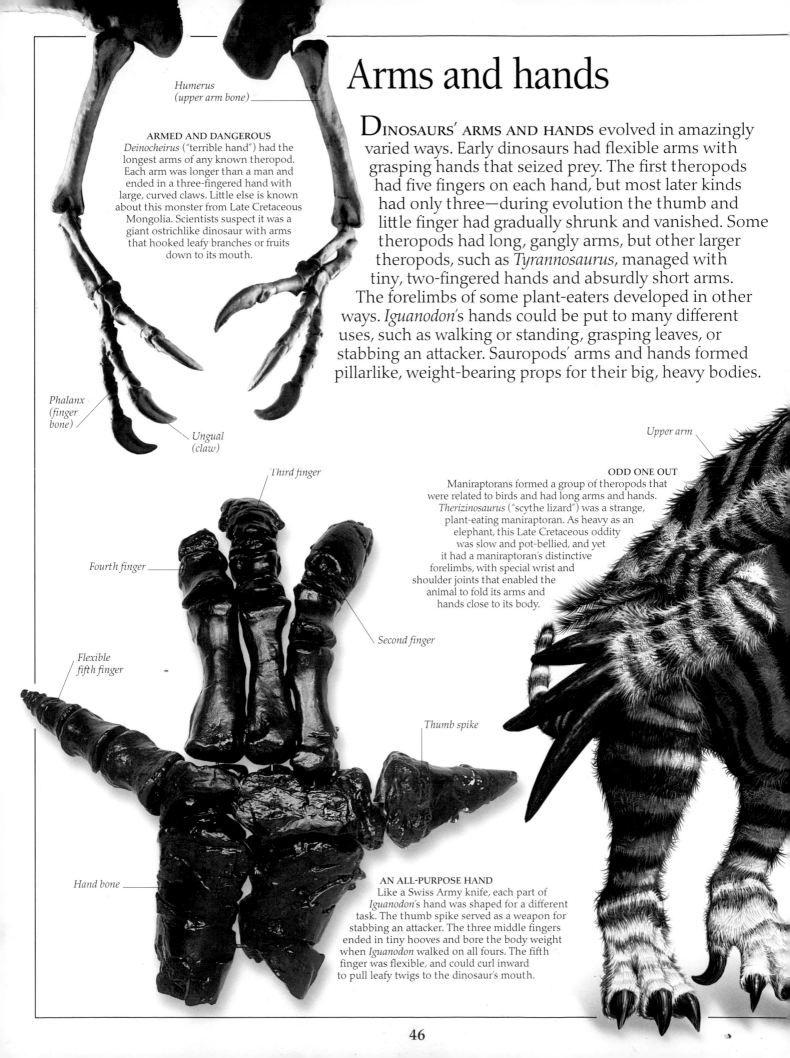

Arms and hands

DINOSAURS' ARMS AND HANDS evolved in amazingly varied ways. Early dinosaurs had flexible arms with grasping hands that seized prey. The first theropods had five fingers on each hand, but most later kinds had only three—during evolution the thumb and little finger had gradually shrunk and vanished. Some theropods had long, gangly arms, but other larger theropods, such as *Tyrannosaurus*, managed with tiny, two-fingered hands and absurdly short arms. The forelimbs of some plant-eaters developed in other ways. *Iguanodon's* hands could be put to many different uses, such as walking or standing, grasping leaves, or stabbing an attacker. Sauropods' arms and hands formed pillarlike, weight-bearing props for their big, heavy bodies.

ARMED AND DANGEROUS
Deinocheirus ("terrible hand") had the longest arms of any known theropod. Each arm was longer than a man and ended in a three-fingered hand with large, curved claws. Little else is known about this monster from Late Cretaceous Mongolia. Scientists suspect it was a giant ostrichlike dinosaur with arms that hooked leafy branches or fruits down to its mouth.

Humerus (upper arm bone)

Phalanx (finger bone)

Ungual (claw)

Third finger

Fourth finger

Flexible fifth finger

Second finger

Upper arm

ODD ONE OUT
Maniraptorans formed a group of theropods that were related to birds and had long arms and hands. *Therizinosaurus* ("scythe lizard") was a strange, plant-eating maniraptoran. As heavy as an elephant, this Late Cretaceous oddity was slow and pot-bellied, and yet it had a maniraptoran's distinctive forelimbs, with special wrist and shoulder joints that enabled the animal to fold its arms and hands close to its body.

Thumb spike

Hand bone

AN ALL-PURPOSE HAND
Like a Swiss Army knife, each part of *Iguanodon's* hand was shaped for a different task. The thumb spike served as a weapon for stabbing an attacker. The three middle fingers ended in tiny hooves and bore the body weight when *Iguanodon* walked on all fours. The fifth finger was flexible, and could curl inward to pull leafy twigs to the dinosaur's mouth.

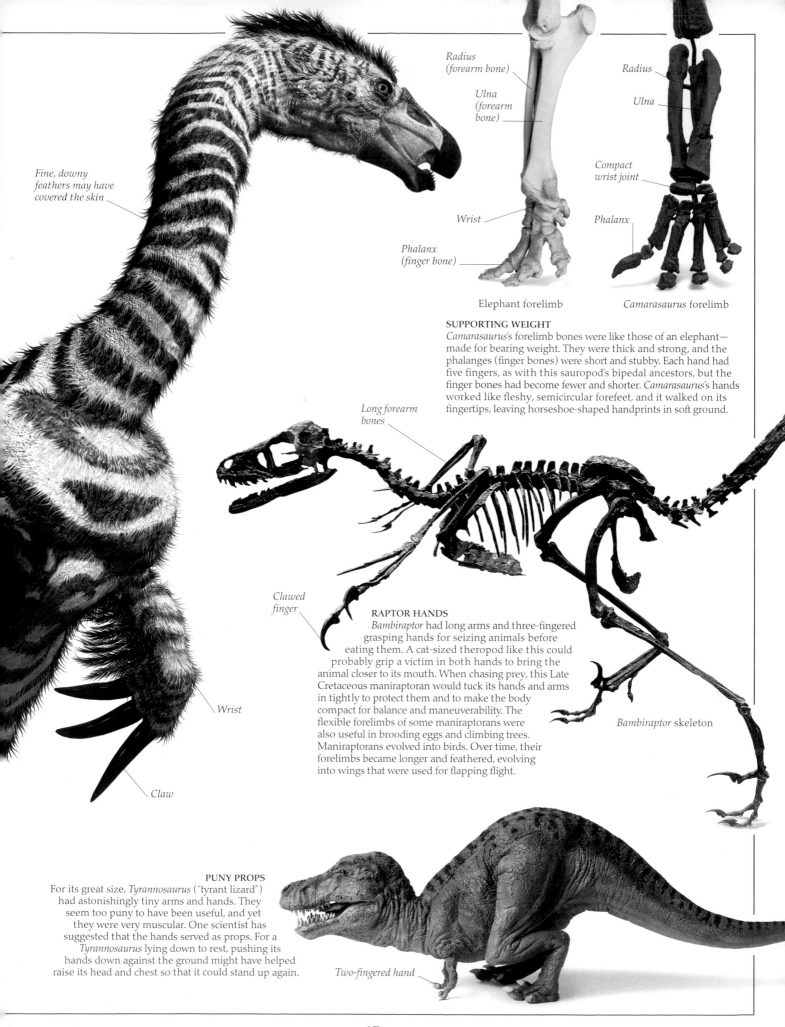

Fine, downy feathers may have covered the skin

Radius (forearm bone)

Ulna (forearm bone)

Wrist

Phalanx (finger bone)

Radius

Ulna

Compact wrist joint

Phalanx

Elephant forelimb

Camarasaurus forelimb

SUPPORTING WEIGHT

Camarasaurus's forelimb bones were like those of an elephant—made for bearing weight. They were thick and strong, and the phalanges (finger bones) were short and stubby. Each hand had five fingers, as with this sauropod's bipedal ancestors, but the finger bones had become fewer and shorter. *Camarasaurus*'s hands worked like fleshy, semicircular forefeet, and it walked on its fingertips, leaving horseshoe-shaped handprints in soft ground.

Long forearm bones

Clawed finger

Wrist

Claw

RAPTOR HANDS

Bambiraptor had long arms and three-fingered grasping hands for seizing animals before eating them. A cat-sized theropod like this could probably grip a victim in both hands to bring the animal closer to its mouth. When chasing prey, this Late Cretaceous maniraptoran would tuck its hands and arms in tightly to protect them and to make the body compact for balance and maneuverability. The flexible forelimbs of some maniraptorans were also useful in brooding eggs and climbing trees. Maniraptorans evolved into birds. Over time, their forelimbs became longer and feathered, evolving into wings that were used for flapping flight.

Bambiraptor skeleton

PUNY PROPS

For its great size, *Tyrannosaurus* ("tyrant lizard") had astonishingly tiny arms and hands. They seem too puny to have been useful, and yet they were very muscular. One scientist has suggested that the hands served as props. For a *Tyrannosaurus* lying down to rest, pushing its hands down against the ground might have helped raise its head and chest so that it could stand up again.

Two-fingered hand

Claws and their uses

Cᴌᴀᴡs ᴄᴀɴ ᴛᴇʟʟ ᴜs ᴍᴜᴄʜ about how dinosaurs lived. Predatory dinosaurs used sharp, curved claws on their narrow fingers as weapons, in the same way that an eagle uses its talons for hunting. When attacking prey, a theropod would hook its claws into the victim's skin and cling on as it bit its prey to death. A group of maniraptorans called dromaeosaurids—including *Deinonychus* and its relatives—were mostly no bigger than a man, and often tackled plant-eaters larger than themselves by savaging their flanks with big, sharp, toe claws. But the longest claws of all belonged to the weird plant-eating theropod, *Therizinosaurus*. Maybe these strange claws helped it to fend off attackers. Most plant-eaters and omnivores (animals that feed on both meat and plants) had no weapons like this. Many had claws that had evolved into short, stubby nails or small hooves to protect the fingers and toes from wear. Some ornithischians may have used their claws for digging up edible plants or burrowing.

Curved claw resembles a fishing hook

Groove where a horny sheath was attached

A FISHY HUNTER

Baryonyx ("heavy claw") gets its name from the large, curved claw on the index finger, or possibly thumb, on each hand. This rhinoceros-sized theropod roamed Europe's rivers, lakes, and swamps early in the Cretaceous Period. Standing at the water's edge, or perhaps wading in, *Baryonyx* might have scooped out large fish with the sudden swipe of a claw. Today, grizzly bears in Alaska catch salmon in a similar way. Or maybe *Baryonyx* seized a fish in its narrow, crocodilelike jaws, and then dug in both claws to prevent its escape.

Baryonyx

Large claw

Three-fingered hand

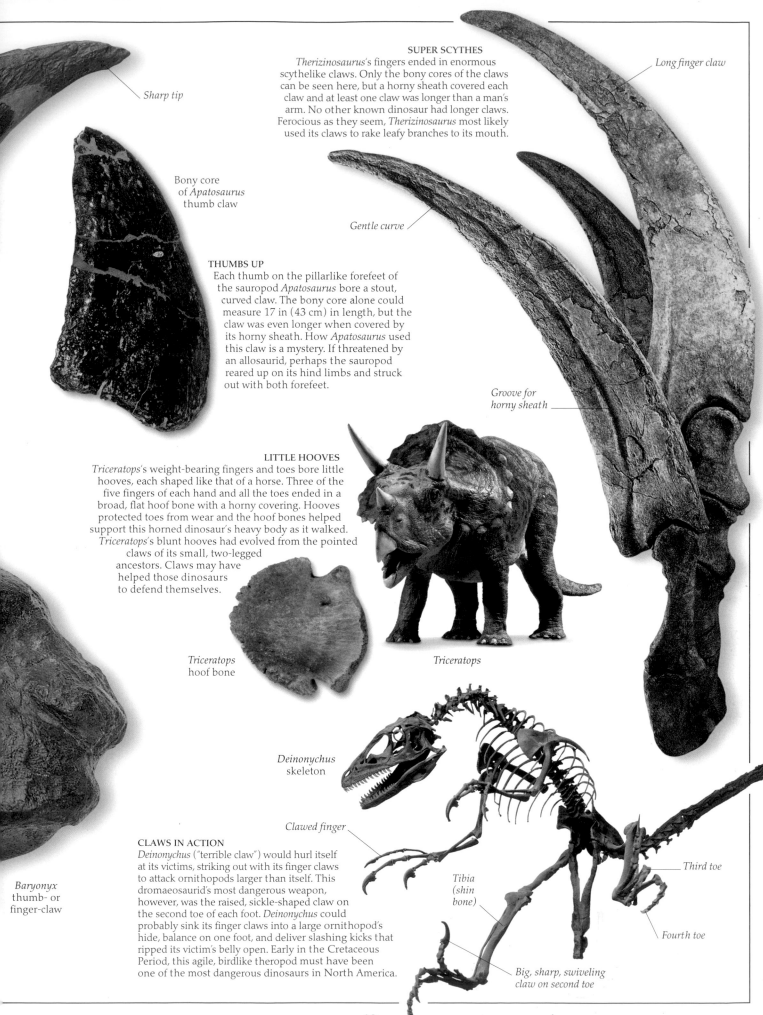

Sharp tip

SUPER SCYTHES
Therizinosaurus's fingers ended in enormous scythelike claws. Only the bony cores of the claws can be seen here, but a horny sheath covered each claw and at least one claw was longer than a man's arm. No other known dinosaur had longer claws. Ferocious as they seem, _Therizinosaurus_ most likely used its claws to rake leafy branches to its mouth.

Long finger claw

Bony core
of _Apatosaurus_
thumb claw

Gentle curve

THUMBS UP
Each thumb on the pillarlike forefeet of the sauropod _Apatosaurus_ bore a stout, curved claw. The bony core alone could measure 17 in (43 cm) in length, but the claw was even longer when covered by its horny sheath. How _Apatosaurus_ used this claw is a mystery. If threatened by an allosaurid, perhaps the sauropod reared up on its hind limbs and struck out with both forefeet.

_Groove for
horny sheath_

LITTLE HOOVES
Triceratops's weight-bearing fingers and toes bore little hooves, each shaped like that of a horse. Three of the five fingers of each hand and all the toes ended in a broad, flat hoof bone with a horny covering. Hooves protected toes from wear and the hoof bones helped support this horned dinosaur's heavy body as it walked. _Triceratops_'s blunt hooves had evolved from the pointed claws of its small, two-legged ancestors. Claws may have helped those dinosaurs to defend themselves.

Triceratops
hoof bone

Triceratops

Deinonychus
skeleton

Clawed finger

CLAWS IN ACTION
Deinonychus ("terrible claw") would hurl itself at its victims, striking out with its finger claws to attack ornithopods larger than itself. This dromaeosaurid's most dangerous weapon, however, was the raised, sickle-shaped claw on the second toe of each foot. _Deinonychus_ could probably sink its finger claws into a large ornithopod's hide, balance on one foot, and deliver slashing kicks that ripped its victim's belly open. Early in the Cretaceous Period, this agile, birdlike theropod must have been one of the most dangerous dinosaurs in North America.

Baryonyx
thumb- or
finger-claw

_Tibia
(shin
bone)_

Third toe

Fourth toe

_Big, sharp, swiveling
claw on second toe_

Legs and feet

FAST-MOVING DINOSAURS' LEGS were much longer than their arms. Theropods and many of the ornithopods they chased walked and ran only on their hind limbs, and not on four legs like horses and other swift animals today. The quickest dinosaurs had slim legs with shins longer than thighs, and long, narrow feet with birdlike toes. In contrast, the heavy, plodding sauropods had thick, strong, weight-bearing legs and short, broad feet. All dinosaurs had vertical legs, each thigh bone fitting into the side of the hip bones through a ball-and-socket joint, similar to those in our hips. And dinosaurs walked on their toes, like dogs, and not flat-footedly, like bears.

Femur (thigh bone)

Tibia (shin bone)

Fibula (calf bone)

Metatarsal (foot bone)

Hypsilophodon hind limb

Toe

BUILT FOR SPEED
Hypsilophodon's long leg bones—tibia (shin bone), fibula (calf bone), metatarsals (foot bones), and phalanges (toe bones)—show that this timid plant-eater could dash away from danger. *Hypsilophodon*'s legs could swing back and forth rapidly during each stride. If it lived now, *Hypsilophodon* would stand no more than waist-high to a man, yet this small ornithopod might outrun an athlete.

Allosaurus

Long, curved neck

Long, bony tail

Ornithomimus

Three-fingered hand on short forelimb

THE GREAT ESCAPE
Ornithomimus ("bird mimic") was a long-legged dinosaur that resembled an ostrich, except for its arms and tail. Such ornithomimids, or ostrich dinosaurs, were theropods with toothless beaks for snacking on plants and small creatures. Speed was their only defense and, like ostriches, a herd of ornithomimids could sprint from danger at up to 40 mph (64 kph).

Ankle joint

Long metatarsal (foot bone)

Phalanx (toe bone)

Ostriches in the Etosha salt pan, Namibia

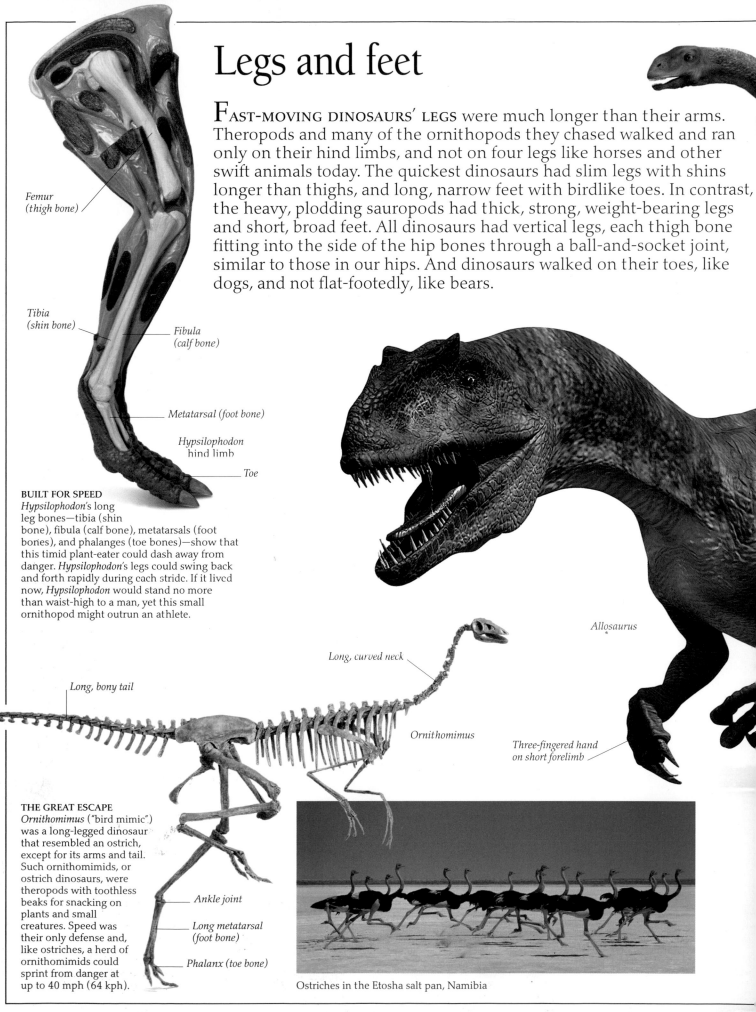

50

PLODDING GIANT
Large sauropods, such as *Vulcanodon*, trudged along very slowly. Their solid limb bones and short shin, foot, and toe bones had evolved not for running, but to support a huge, heavy body. Most sauropods did not need to run fast. They were large enough to ignore most theropod predators.

Vulcanodon

Pillarlike limb

Tibia

High ankle joint

Long metatarsal

Phalanx

Hallux

Massive tibia

Short metatarsal

Low ankle joint

Phalanx

THEROPOD'S FOOT
Predatory dinosaurs get their collective name—theropods ("beast feet")—from their sharp, curved claws, like those on this *Tyrannosaurus* foot. A typical theropod foot had three main, forward-pointing toes, and a little hallux (big toe) that had evolved into a spur (spike) at the back of the foot, and was too short to touch the ground.

SAUROPOD'S FOOT
Diplodocus's hind limbs were thick and strong to bear its heavy weight. Each of the pillarlike legs rested on a broad, five-toed foot. Like other dinosaurs, sauropods walked on their toes, but beneath the toe and foot bones lay supporting fibrous heels. The legs and feet of a sauropod resembled an elephant's.

Powerful thigh

ON THE RUN
Some scientists think that *Allosaurus*'s powerful legs drove this predator along at up to 20 mph (32 kph) when it was chasing prey. But a large and short-armed theropod, such as an *Allosaurus*, risked serious injury if it fell while running fast. Perhaps this explains signs of breakage and mending in 14 ribs in a skeleton of an *Allosaurus*. Or maybe the ribs were damaged in some other way? Many scientists do not believe that this theropod's legs were capable of speeds greater than a human jogger.

High ankle

Weight-bearing toes

Ancient footprints

A DINOSAUR WALKING by a river, lake, or sea sometimes left its footprints in soft mud that quickly dried and hardened. Buried by successive layers of mud, this slowly turned to rock, preserving the footprints inside it as fossils. The shapes and sizes of such prints and the gaps between them can help scientists to identify different types of track-makers, and also work out the sizes of the dinosaurs and how fast they walked or ran. Scientists can even tell where a dinosaur hunted, or where a herd trekked together. People find fossil dinosaur tracks all over the world. They give us glimpses of dinosaurs' lives that we could never get by just studying their bones.

THUNDER FOOT
This fossil sauropod footprint dwarfs a human hand. Parallel rows of washtub-sized depressions like this one pockmark rocks at Purgatoire in Colorado. They tell us that a herd of diplodocid dinosaurs (huge sauropods with a long neck and long tail) passed by some time late in the Jurassic Period. Scientists were not sure precisely which dinosaur made the gigantic Purgatoire prints, so they gave it a special name—*Brontopodus*, meaning "thunder foot."

Inner toe print

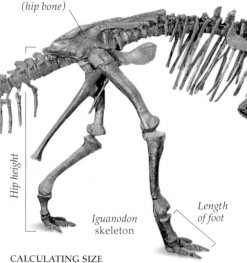

Ilium (hip bone)

Hip height

Iguanodon skeleton

Length of foot

CALCULATING SIZE
An *Iguanodon* might have measured anything from 26 to 40 ft (8–12 m) in length. Scientists can estimate a dinosaur's size from just its footprints, without even seeing its fossil bones. Multiplying the size of a footprint by four gives an idea of the dinosaur's hip height. Scientists can then work out the likely length of the whole animal.

FOSSIL TRACKS
Dinosaurs left behind more fossil footprints than fossil bones. Scientists have identified 150,000 tracks in a square patch of land, half a mile (1 km) across, at a site in Wyoming. Dinosaurs churned up the ground so heavily that tracing individual footprints can be impossible. Even where prints show up clearly, some can be misleading. As shown here, the survival of only the hindfeet prints of a four-legged dinosaur might incorrectly suggest that they came from a two-legged dinosaur.

Small dinosaur's hindfeet leave lighter impressions on mud

Mudflat

Wet surface layer of mud

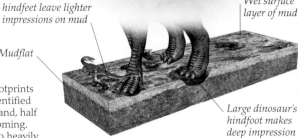

Large dinosaur's hindfoot makes deep impression

1 MAKING FOOTPRINTS
A small two-legged dinosaur and large four-legged dinosaur are seen crossing a mudflat. Both leave footprints on the surface, but only the large dinosaur's hindfeet are heavy enough to make dents in the firmer layer of mud lying beneath.

Outer toe print

CLOVER LEAF CLUE
Fossil footprints shaped like a clover leaf
often crop up in the Early Cretaceous
rocks of southern England, and belong
to blunt-toed *Iguanodon*. At 11½ in
(29 cm) long, this particular print was
made by a young *Iguanodon* weighing
roughly half a ton. Larger adults
were four times heavier and made
footprints three times as long as
this one. The narrow tracks of
Iguanodon and other dinosaurs
prove that dinosaurs walked
with limbs erect, not
sprawling like
other reptiles.

Iguanodon
footprint

*Impression of
middle toe*

WHERE HUNTERS RAN
A hunting pack of *Dilophosaurus* very likely made these three-toed
tracks in Arizona, some time early in the Jurassic Period. These
theropods were very agile, and adults measured 20 ft (6 m) in length.
The longer a dinosaur's stride, the faster it ran. By measuring stride
length and hip height, scientists have worked out that *Dilophosaurus*
could chase its prey at up to 23½ mph (37.8 kph).

*Convex
impression of large
dinosaur's hindfoot*

*No impressions of
small dinosaur*

*Flood waters
swirl in*

*Flood waters
subsiding*

*Fresh mud
deposited*

*Top layer of mud
lifted and swirled
away by current*

*Firmer layer of
mud left intact*

*Impression of
hindfoot filled in*

2 LOSING FOOTPRINTS
A nearby river overflows its banks while the
footprints are still fresh. Water streams across the
mudflat and scours away all the footprints that have
just been made in the soft surface mud. Only the
underprints formed in the underlying mud survive.

3 FOOTPRINTS FOSSILIZED
When the flood subsides, it leaves a smooth layer
of mud covering the underprints. Over millions of
years, more floods dump fresh mud in layers that
get compressed and harden into sedimentary rock.
Inside, the underprints survive as fossils.

4 FOSSIL PRINTS REVEALED
Erosion causes the fossil-bearing rock to appear
on the surface. Splitting it between two layers
reveals the hidden fossil prints. Since only hindfeet
prints survive, anyone but an expert would assume
that a two-legged dinosaur had made them.

Tough skins

A TYPICAL DINOSAUR'S SKIN was scaly and waterproof, and similar to a lizard's or crocodile's. It protected the dinosaur's body from drying and shriveling up in hot, dry conditions. The skin was also tough, so it was not easily cut if the dinosaur fell or was injured in a fight. Ankylosaurs and some sauropods had skins with bony armor for extra protection—a theropod biting into their hides risked breaking its teeth. Scientists learn all this from the fossil impressions left by the skins of some dinosaurs, but we can only guess at the colors of the skin. It is very likely, big dinosaurs were as drab as an elephant, but perhaps small dinosaurs were brightly colored for display or for camouflage.

Bright pattern on skin

REPTILIAN SKIN
The skin of most lizards has flat scales that overlap like roof tiles, but the Gila monster's skin is covered in bumpy scales arranged like tiny, close-set pebbles. From skin impressions preserved in rocks, we know that dinosaurs had scales like this. On parts of their bodies, large and small scales formed mosaic patterns.

Pea-sized ossicles (bony lumps)

Saltasaurus

Armored hide

COAT OF ARMOR
The backs and flanks (sides) of *Saltasaurus*, and some other dinosaurs in a group of sauropods called titanosaurs, were fortified with layers of flexible armor. Set into their hides were thousands of bony lumps ranging in size from peas to dinner plates. Here and there, ridged bony plates as big as the palm of a human hand reinforced the skin.

Saltasaurus skin impression

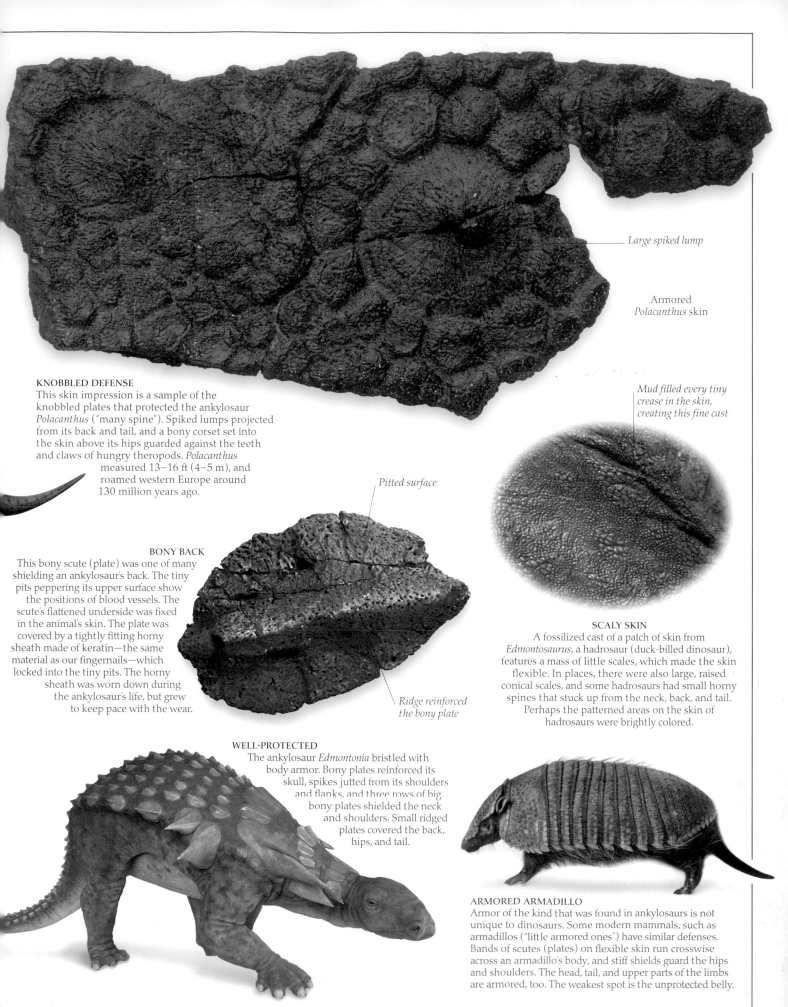

Large spiked lump

Armored
Polacanthus skin

KNOBBLED DEFENSE
This skin impression is a sample of the
knobbled plates that protected the ankylosaur
Polacanthus ("many spine"). Spiked lumps projected
from its back and tail, and a bony corset set into
the skin above its hips guarded against the teeth
and claws of hungry theropods. _Polacanthus_
measured 13–16 ft (4–5 m), and
roamed western Europe around
130 million years ago.

_Mud filled every tiny
crease in the skin,
creating this fine cast_

Pitted surface

BONY BACK
This bony scute (plate) was one of many
shielding an ankylosaur's back. The tiny
pits peppering its upper surface show
the positions of blood vessels. The
scute's flattened underside was fixed
in the animal's skin. The plate was
covered by a tightly fitting horny
sheath made of keratin—the same
material as our fingernails—which
locked into the tiny pits. The horny
sheath was worn down during
the ankylosaur's life, but grew
to keep pace with the wear.

_Ridge reinforced
the bony plate_

SCALY SKIN
A fossilized cast of a patch of skin from
Edmontosaurus, a hadrosaur (duck-billed dinosaur),
features a mass of little scales, which made the skin
flexible. In places, there were also large, raised
conical scales, and some hadrosaurs had small horny
spines that stuck up from the neck, back, and tail.
Perhaps the patterned areas on the skin of
hadrosaurs were brightly colored.

WELL-PROTECTED
The ankylosaur _Edmontonia_ bristled with
body armor. Bony plates reinforced its
skull, spikes jutted from its shoulders
and flanks, and three rows of big
bony plates shielded the neck
and shoulders. Small ridged
plates covered the back,
hips, and tail.

ARMORED ARMADILLO
Armor of the kind that was found in ankylosaurs is not
unique to dinosaurs. Some modern mammals, such as
armadillos ("little armored ones") have similar defenses.
Bands of scutes (plates) on flexible skin run crosswise
across an armadillo's body, and stiff shields guard the hips
and shoulders. The head, tail, and upper parts of the limbs
are armored, too. The weakest spot is the unprotected belly.

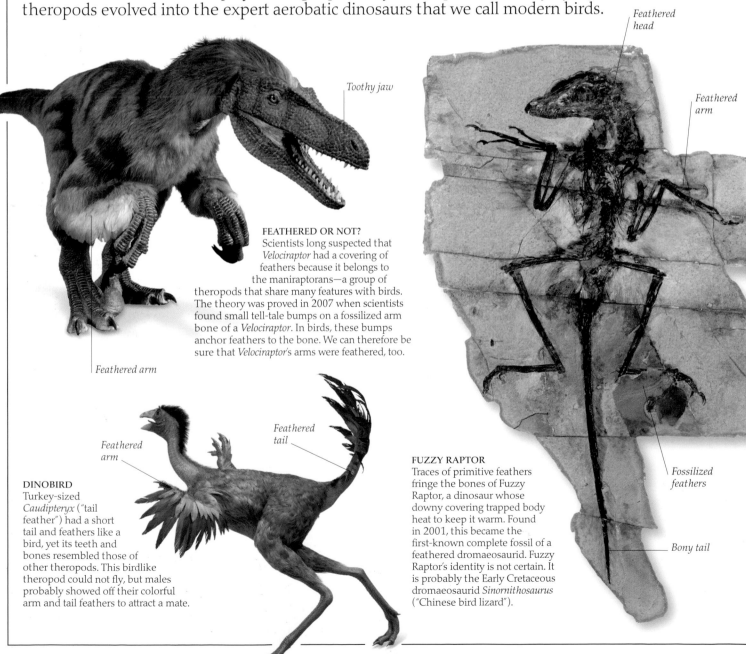

Feathered dinosaurs

Not all dinosaurs had scaly skin—the skin of some was covered in down or feathers. The first evidence came in 1861 when a German scientist described *Archaeopteryx*, a primitive bird with wings, but a long, bony tail, clawed fingers, and teeth like those of theropods. In 1996, Chinese paleontologists discovered *Sinosauropteryx*, a small birdlike dinosaur with "dinofuzz"—a downy covering on its body. Then came more exciting finds—theropods with showy feathers and feathered arms that worked as wings for gliding, not flapping. The first featherlike structures were downy and were probably used for keeping the body warm. Feathers used for display and flight probably developed later. Early flying theropods evolved into the expert aerobatic dinosaurs that we call modern birds.

Feathered head

Feathered arm

Toothy jaw

FEATHERED OR NOT?
Scientists long suspected that *Velociraptor* had a covering of feathers because it belongs to the maniraptorans—a group of theropods that share many features with birds. The theory was proved in 2007 when scientists found small tell-tale bumps on a fossilized arm bone of a *Velociraptor*. In birds, these bumps anchor feathers to the bone. We can therefore be sure that *Velociraptor*'s arms were feathered, too.

Feathered arm

Feathered arm

Feathered tail

DINOBIRD
Turkey-sized *Caudipteryx* ("tail feather") had a short tail and feathers like a bird, yet its teeth and bones resembled those of other theropods. This birdlike theropod could not fly, but males probably showed off their colorful arm and tail feathers to attract a mate.

FUZZY RAPTOR
Traces of primitive feathers fringe the bones of Fuzzy Raptor, a dinosaur whose downy covering trapped body heat to keep it warm. Found in 2001, this became the first-known complete fossil of a feathered dromaeosaurid. Fuzzy Raptor's identity is not certain. It is probably the Early Cretaceous dromaeosaurid *Sinornithosaurus* ("Chinese bird lizard").

Fossilized feathers

Bony tail

Wing with long flight feathers

TAKING TO THE SKY

Technically, all birds are dinosaurs, but some early birds were more similar to ground-based dinosaurs than they were to modern birds. *Archaeopteryx* ("ancient feather" or "ancient wing") had the feathered wings of a flying bird, yet the claws, hips, legs, toothy jaws, and bony tail of a small theropod. Late in the Jurassic Period, this crow-sized prehistoric bird flapped over semidesert islands in what is now southern Germany.

Archaeopteryx

Toothy jaw

Feathered tail

Forelimbs may have supported flight feathers

Feather impressions

Archaeopteryx fossil

CLIMBERS AND GLIDERS

Epidexipteryx ("display feather") was a tiny, feathered maniraptoran that probably climbed and leaped around in trees. Some scientists believe it glided from tree to tree, using feathered arms as wings. This Jurassic proto-bird (dinosaur with basic features of a bird) lived before *Archaeopteryx*, which flew by flapping its wings. Flight by gliding was probably followed by flapping flight.

A BIRD WITH A BEAK

Confuciusornis had more features in common with modern birds than do earlier birds, such as *Archaeopteryx*. *Confuciusornis* had a horny beak and a pygostyle (a bony tail core formed from fused tail bones). This helped it to fly better than *Archaeopteryx*, yet *Confuciusornis* still had some primitive features, such as clawed wing fingers. It lived in Early Cretaceous China and bred in colonies.

Flight feathers on wing

Clawed wing finger

Toothless beak

Leading edge

Feather shaft

FLIGHT FEATHERS

We know that *Archaeopteryx* could fly because the primary feathers (feathers that are the most important for flapping flight) on its wings were shaped like this one from a modern flying bird. The flight feather's shaft is closer to one edge than the other. The primary feathers of flightless birds are shaped very differently—each feather's shaft runs through the middle. This was characteristic of flightless feathered dinosaurs such as *Caudipteryx* as well.

Long tail feather

Highly curved foot claw

Eggs and young

DINOSAURS HATCHED FROM HARD-SHELLED eggs like those of birds and crocodiles. By studying a fossil eggshell's shape and texture, paleontologists can tell which type of dinosaur laid the egg. Sometimes they even find a tiny skeleton inside the fossil egg. Such discoveries include the remains of whole nesting colonies of hadrosaurs and sauropods. Small dinosaurs probably sat on their eggs to warm them as birds do, but big dinosaurs hatched their eggs with warmth from sunshine or rotting vegetation. Some dinosaurs ran around and started looking for food soon after emerging from eggs. Others needed parental care. Most kinds of dinosaur grew fast. A *Tyrannosaurus* that hatched from an egg no bigger than a loaf of bread weighed as much as 65 lb (30 kg) by the time it was two. By 14, this theropod weighed about 1.9 tons (1.7 metric tons), and more than twice that by 18. But it did not live long: by 30, the *Tyrannosaurus* was dead.

A GIANT'S EGGS

Sauropods' cannonball-shaped eggs measured about 5 in (13 cm) across. Each occupied the space of a dozen chicken eggs. A thick shell protected the egg from breakage and tiny holes in the shell let air reach the embryo inside. These eggs seem small for the size of the huge plant-eating dinosaurs that laid them, but much larger eggs would have needed shells so thick that hatchlings could not have broken out.

Damage caused during fossilization

READY TO HATCH

Tiny bones found in a fossil egg helped a modelmaker to create this lifelike restoration of a *Troodon* about to hatch. Such eggs have been found at Egg Mountain, a Late Cretaceous fossil site in the northwest of Montana. *Troodon* mothers laid eggs two at a time. Incubated upright in the ground, their clutches hatched out into babies that quickly ran around. Fossils of young and adult dinosaurs found together make it likely that the hatchlings formed part of family groups.

Head tucked in

Tail tucked under body

Elongated shape

STOLEN GOODS?

Oviraptor and its relatives—the oviraptorids—laid narrow, hard-shelled eggs like this one, discovered in Mongolia. These eggs are typically 7 in (18 cm) long. *Oviraptor* means "egg thief." Scientists once thought that a small ceratopsian called *Protoceratops* laid the eggs and that *Oviraptor* used to steal them. The scientists realized their mistake only when paleontologists found fossils of another oviraptorid sitting on similar eggs.

DINO KIDS

This realistic model shows *Maiasaura* hatchlings crouching in the protection of their mud-mound nest among unhatched eggs. *Maiasaura* was a large hadrosaur (duck-billed dinosaur) and dozens of individuals nested close together. Like birds, the mothers fed their babies in the nests until they were strong enough to leave. This habit earned this dinosaur its name, which means "good mother lizard."

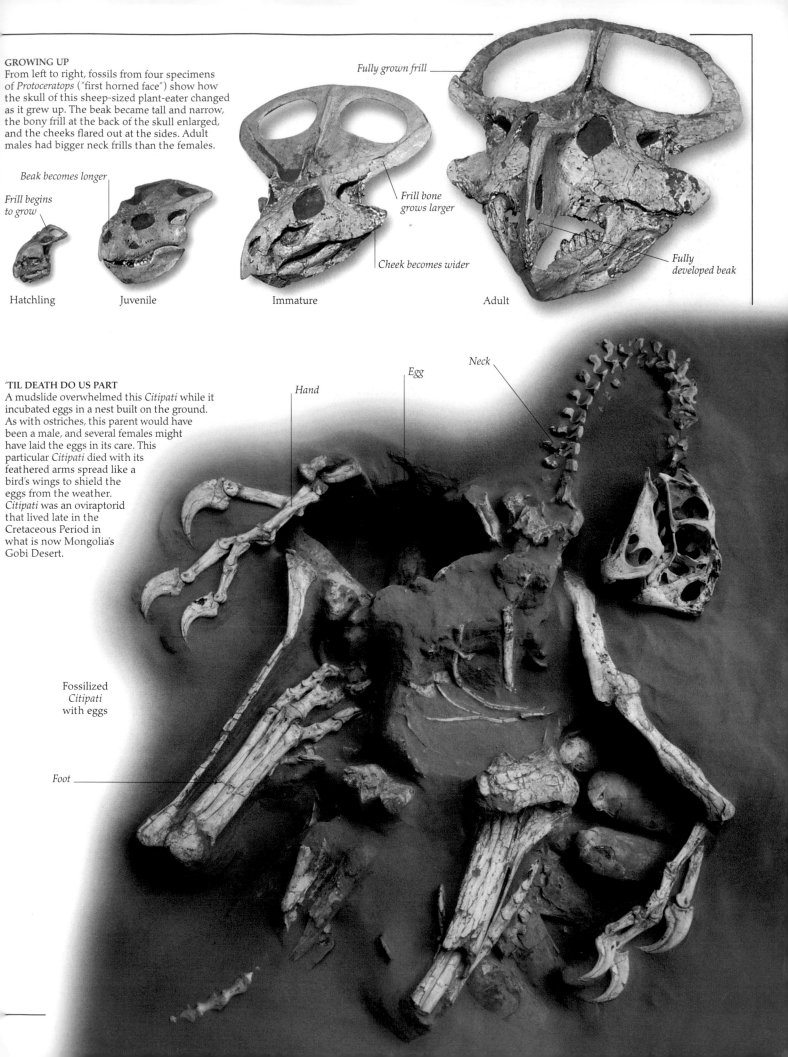

GROWING UP
From left to right, fossils from four specimens of *Protoceratops* ("first horned face") show how the skull of this sheep-sized plant-eater changed as it grew up. The beak became tall and narrow, the bony frill at the back of the skull enlarged, and the cheeks flared out at the sides. Adult males had bigger neck frills than the females.

Fully grown frill

Beak becomes longer

Frill begins to grow

Frill bone grows larger

Cheek becomes wider

Fully developed beak

Hatchling

Juvenile

Immature

Adult

'TIL DEATH DO US PART
A mudslide overwhelmed this *Citipati* while it incubated eggs in a nest built on the ground. As with ostriches, this parent would have been a male, and several females might have laid the eggs in its care. This particular *Citipati* died with its feathered arms spread like a bird's wings to shield the eggs from the weather. *Citipati* was an oviraptorid that lived late in the Cretaceous Period in what is now Mongolia's Gobi Desert.

Hand

Egg

Neck

Fossilized *Citipati* with eggs

Foot

Finding dinosaur fossils

How do fossil hunters discover the remains of dinosaurs? First, they look for the right kinds of fossil-bearing rocks. Sedimentary rocks like sandstones that date from the Age of Dinosaurs often show up most clearly in badlands (barren and eroded regions), deserts, cliffs, and quarries. Paleontologists search these places for unusual rock. What we might consider shiny or spongy stones may be recognized by the experts as scraps of dinosaur fossils—pieces that may have broken off from a larger fossil such as a skull. Discovery is just the start. A team of experts may work for weeks to free a large fossil from its rocky tomb without damaging it. Meanwhile, they measure, map, and photograph each bone.

ANCIENT TREASURE TROVE
A sauropodomorph skeleton dwarfs this paleontologist working at a dinosaur dig in China's Lufeng Basin, a bowl-shaped region filled with sedimentary rocks. In 1938, Chinese paleontologist Yang Zhongjian unearthed fossils of the prosauropod *Lufengosaurus*, the first dinosaur to be found here. Since then, the area's sandstones, mudstones, and shales have yielded more than 100 dinosaur skeletons dating from the Jurassic Period.

THE HUNT
Secured by a safety rope, paleontologist Hans Larsson perches precariously halfway up a cliff to excavate a toe bone of *Centrosaurus*, a horned dinosaur. This scene is set in the remote badlands of Dinosaur Provincial Park in Alberta, Canada, but the hunt for dinosaurs ranges from frozen Antarctica to the baking sands of the Sahara Desert.

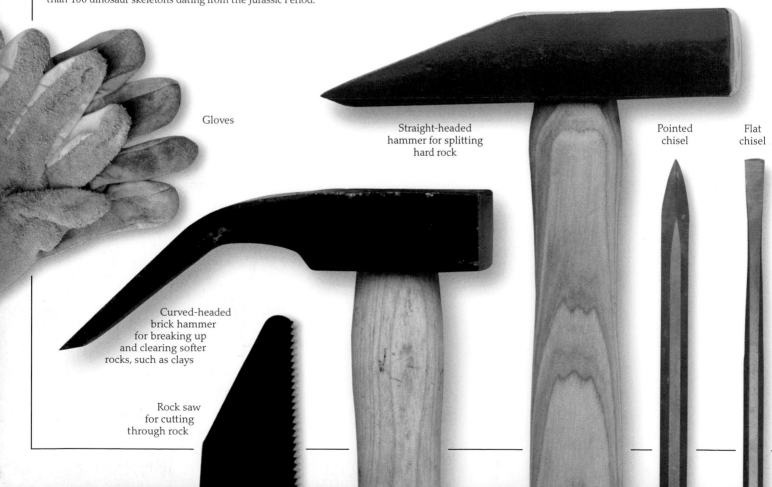

Gloves

Straight-headed hammer for splitting hard rock

Pointed chisel

Flat chisel

Curved-headed brick hammer for breaking up and clearing softer rocks, such as clays

Rock saw for cutting through rock

THE FIND

When excavating the bones of a dinosaur, the paleontologists first remove the bulk of rocks around the bones. Then they clear away the matrix (rocky material immediately surrounding the bones) as much as possible using hammers and chisels. Next they encase the bones in jackets made of sackcloth soaked in wet plaster. This sets hard quickly, forming a strong, rigid coat. Each plaster jacket protects the fragile fossil bone inside against damage on the ride to a laboratory for proper study.

1 CLEANING A LIMB BONE
A paleontologist carefully brushes away dirt from a big, fragile dinosaur limb bone. The goal is to clean the fossil before encasing it in plaster.

2 MAKING A PLASTER CAST
The paleontologists apply runny plaster of Paris to sackcloth bandages. They wrap these around the bone and wait for the plaster to set hard.

3 PREPARING FOR STUDY
The dinosaur bone arrives at a laboratory still wrapped in its plaster cast. Technicians remove the cast so the bone can be studied.

TOOLS OF THE TRADE

Paleontologists use tools like these to free fossils stuck in rock, to clean them, and to pack them safely for later examination. They might paint fragile bones with watery glue to stop them from crumbling, and then encase the bones in a jacket. They make one kind of jacket by dipping an open-weave fabric into a paste made of water mixed with powdered plaster of Paris. Or they might wrap the bones in aluminum foil and then pour on chemicals producing polyurethane foam, which expands and covers the fossils to protect them.

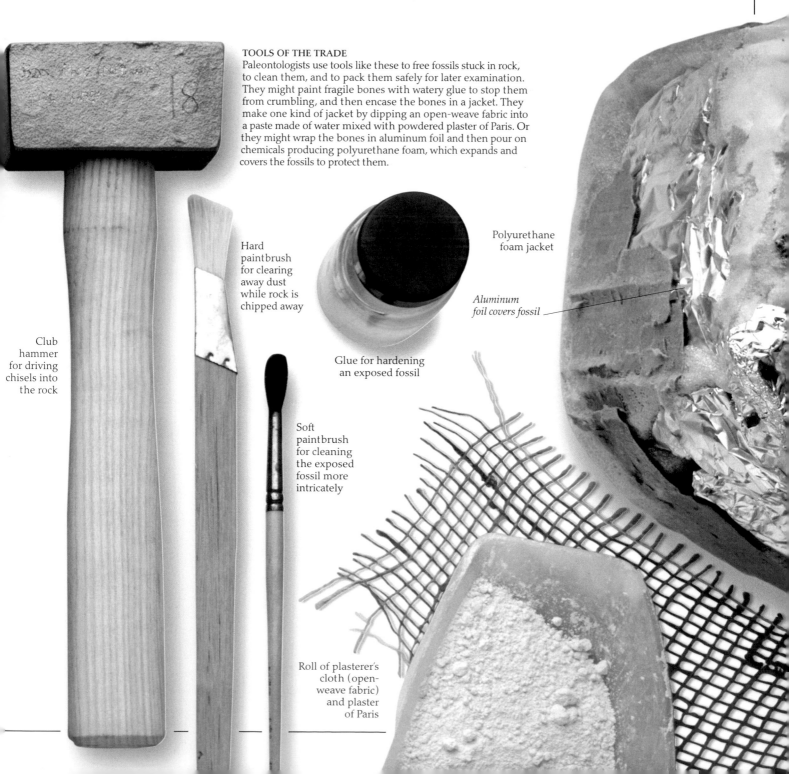

Hard paintbrush for clearing away dust while rock is chipped away

Polyurethane foam jacket

Aluminum foil covers fossil

Glue for hardening an exposed fossil

Club hammer for driving chisels into the rock

Soft paintbrush for cleaning the exposed fossil more intricately

Roll of plasterer's cloth (open-weave fabric) and plaster of Paris

Rebuilding a dinosaur

DIGGING UP A DINOSAUR'S bones is just the first step toward learning what it looked like and putting it on show. Inside a museum laboratory, technicians called preparators start by sawing off the plaster jackets protecting the bones. If the bones are embedded in rock, the next step is to extract them carefully. Preparators chip away hard rock with chisels. They use powered tools like dentists' drills for detailed work, and even acid for removing certain kinds of stone from around the fossils. Once the bones are cleaned, paleontologists can reconstruct the dinosaur's skeleton by fitting them together. Modelmakers can then be guided by paleontologists in building a lifelike restoration of the animal, using bumps and ridges on the bones as clues to where muscles and other tissues were attached.

EXPOSING THE FOSSIL
A technician uses dilute acetic acid to expose embryos hidden in fossil dinosaur eggs. Each day, acid eats away a wafer-thin layer of the stony material around the embryos without harming their frail bones, which have a different chemical composition. Washing and drying the embryos is part of this process, which can last up to a year.

Ligament scar

Cartilage cap of ankle joint

FINDING CLUES
Fossil bones can tell us about muscles and other tissues that have vanished. The upper end of this third metatarsal (foot) bone of an *Iguanodon* is roughened and shows where cartilage (gristle) protected the ankle joint. The bottom end is where cartilage protected this bone against the first phalanx (toe bone). A scar marks where a ligament joined this bone to the fourth metatarsal bone.

Cartilage surface of joint for first phalanx

ON DISPLAY
A cast of a *Diplodocus* skeleton forms the centerpiece in the main hall of London's Natural History Museum. Museums worldwide display replicas of dinosaur skeletons. The replicas are cast from molds made from real fossils, many of them unique and too fragile to be put on display.

FLESH AND BONES
This model shows a freshly dead *Baryonyx* lying on the bottom of a lake. A sculptor made this realistic model by studying the way the dinosaur's bones were arranged when paleontologists dug them up. Scientists and the modelmaker then worked out where to add muscles, skin, and other tissues that would bulk out the body.

DIGITAL DINOS

Special 3-D modeling and graphics computer software allow graphic artists to create highly detailed digital models of dinosaurs. They first draw a body framework in the software and bulk it out. Next, they add details such as tint and texture to the skin or surface of the model. Artists with expert anatomical knowledge can manipulate a model to pose a dinosaur in different ways and even make it move in various environments under simulated lighting.

Digital model
of *Corythosaurus*

*Reconstruction
of lake bed*

Baryonyx
restoration

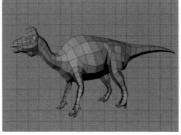

1 BASE MESH
The first step is to make a mesh that forms the base or starting point of the model. An accurate drawing of the dinosaur's skeleton guides the artist in building the dinosaur's basic shape from a grid made of polygons.

2 SHAPING THE DINOSAUR
Computer software subdivides the basic polygons into millions of smaller units. An artist can then sculpt these units as a kind of digital clay, modifying them to refine the dinosaur's shape.

3 CORRECTING INACCURACIES
While making the digital model, it is important to correct mistakes that are often present in traditional models of dinosaurs. For instance, a hadrosaur such as *Corythosaurus* is now known to have a skin crest behind its head.

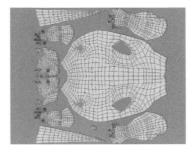

4 UV MAPPING
3-D painting tools add basic color details to the model. But the artist also uses a technique called UV mapping to cut the dinosaur's skin into pieces. These are placed on a virtual canvas to add finer details of color and texture.

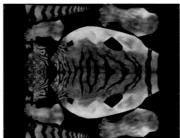

5 ADDING COLOR
The bits of skin are spread out on the flat canvas like pieces of animal hide pinned onto a table. Working on these, the artist creates detailed color maps that consist of tints, shades, and tones of different colors.

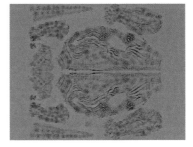

6 ADDING MORE DETAIL
UV mapping also adds details such as texture or shininess. It can make one part of a dinosaur's body appear to be glossier or scalier than another, making the dinosaur look more real.

7 RIGGING
To pose or animate the dinosaur, a rigging artist, who is an expert in anatomy, creates a digital skeleton and digital muscles that will convincingly move and bend the digital animal.

8 RENDERING
In this step, the flat maps created earlier are applied to the model. The dinosaur is then placed in a simulated environment and is illuminated by virtual sources of light.

63

Classification of dinosaurs

EACH KIND OF DINOSAUR is called a species, and one or more related species make up a genus (plural, genera). A species together with all of its descendants forms a group called a clade. A diagram made up of clades is known as a cladogram. Our cladogram shows how most main groups of dinosaur were related. For instance, the species *Tyrannosaurus rex* belongs in the successively larger clades of *Tyrannosaurus*, tyrannosaurs, coelurosaurs, tetanurans, theropods, and saurischians.

PIONEERS OF CLASSIFICATION
In 1735, Sweden's Carl Linnaeus classified living things into species and genera. In 1887, Britain's Harry Govier Seeley (above) classified dinosaurs as ornithischians and saurischians. In 1950, Germany's Willi Hennig began developing cladistics—the system of grouping species and their descendants into clades.

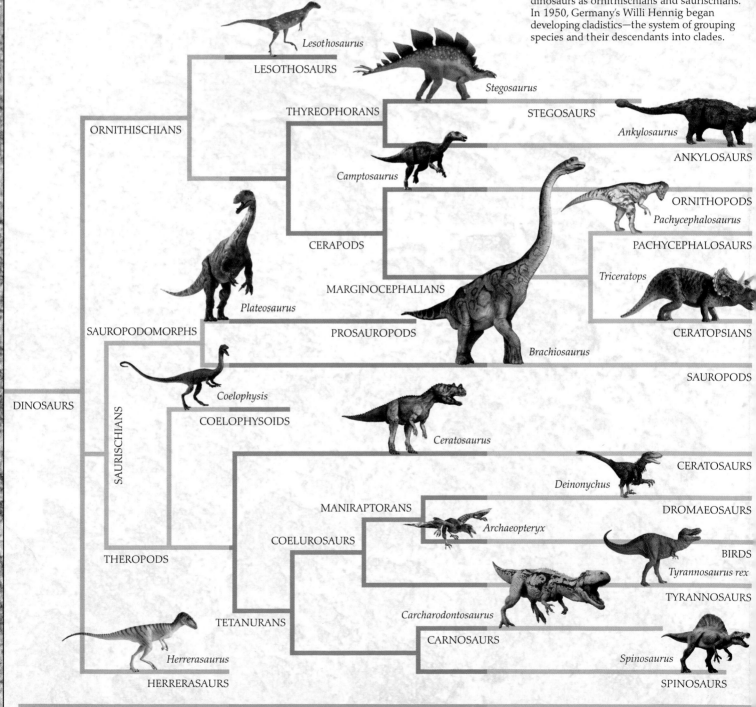

Lesothosaurus

LESOTHOSAURS

Stegosaurus

THYREOPHORANS

STEGOSAURS

ORNITHISCHIANS

Ankylosaurus

ANKYLOSAURS

Camptosaurus

ORNITHOPODS

Pachycephalosaurus

CERAPODS

PACHYCEPHALOSAURS

Triceratops

MARGINOCEPHALIANS

SAUROPODOMORPHS

Plateosaurus

PROSAUROPODS

CERATOPSIANS

Brachiosaurus

SAUROPODS

DINOSAURS

Coelophysis

COELOPHYSOIDS

Ceratosaurus

SAURISCHIANS

CERATOSAURS

Deinonychus

MANIRAPTORANS

DROMAEOSAURS

Archaeopteryx

COELUROSAURS

BIRDS

THEROPODS

Tyrannosaurus rex

TYRANNOSAURS

Carcharodontosaurus

TETANURANS

CARNOSAURS

Herrerasaurus

Spinosaurus

HERRERASAURS

SPINOSAURS

TRIASSIC (250–200 mya)	JURASSIC (200–145 mya)	CRETACEOUS (145–65 mya)

Pronunciation guide

NAMING DINOSAURS
Most dinosaurs' scientific names are based on Latin or Greek words and each name means something. For instance, *Triceratops* ("three-horned face") describes a special anatomical feature. *Eocursor* ("dawn runner") describes this ornithopod's behavior. *Argentinosaurus* tells us where this sauropod's fossils were found. *Barsboldia*'s name honors the Mongolian paleontologist Rinchen Barsbold. Many names are tricky to say, but our syllable-by-syllable guide helps you pronounce many of those in the book.

NAME	PRONUNCIATION
Albertosaurus	al BERT oh SORE uss
Allosaurus	allo SORE uss
Alxasaurus	AL shah SORE uss
Amargasaurus	ah MAHR gah SORE uss
Anchisaurus	ankee SORE uss
Ankylosaurus	an KEE loh SORE uss
Apatosaurus	a PAT oh SORE uss
Archaeopteryx	AR kee OP terricks
Argentinosaurus	AR jen TEEN oh SORE uss
Bambiraptor	BAM bee RAP tor
Barapasaurus	buh RAH pah SORE uss
Barosaurus	barrow SORE uss
Barsboldia	bahrs BOHL dee a
Baryonyx	barry ON icks
Brachiosaurus	brackee oh SORE uss
Camarasaurus	KAM a ra SORE uss
Camptosaurus	KAMP toe SORE uss
Carcharodontosaurus	kar KAR oh DON toe SORE uss
Carnotaurus	kar noh TOR uss
Caudipteryx	kor DIP terricks
Centrosaurus	SEN troh SORE uss
Ceratosaurus	seh rat oh SORE uss
Citipati	CHIT i puh tih
Coelophysis	SEE low FYE siss
Compsognathus	KOMP sog NAY thuss
Confuciusornis	CON FYOO shi SOR nis
Corythosaurus	ko RITH oh SORE uss
Cryolophosaurus	KREE o LOAF o SORE uss
Deinocheirus	DIE no KIRE uss
Deinonychus	die NON ee kuss
Dilophosaurus	die LOAF oh SORE uss
Diplodocus	di PLOD o kuss
Dryosaurus	DRY oh SORE uss
Edmontonia	ED mon TOE nee a
Edmontosaurus	ed MON toe SORE uss
Eocursor	EE oh KER sor
Eoraptor	EE oh RAP tor
Epidexipteryx	epi dex IP terricks
Euoplocephalus	YOU owe ploh SEFF a luss
Gallimimus	gally MEEM uss
Gastonia	gass TOE nee a
Giganotosaurus	jig anno toe SORE uss
Guanlong	gwahn LOONG
Herrerasaurus	he RAIR a SORE uss
Heterodontosaurus	HET er oh DONT oh SORE uss
Huayangosaurus	HWAH YAHNG oh SORE uss
Hypsilophodon	HIP sill OFF o don
Iguanodon	ig WAHN o don

NAME	PRONUNCIATION
Kentrosaurus	KEN troh SORE uss
Lambeosaurus	LAMB ee oh SORE uss
Leaellynasaura	lee EL in a SORE a
Lesothosaurus	le SUE too SORE uss
Maiasaura	MY a SORE a
Majungatholus	mah JOONG gah THOL uss
Mamenchisaurus	ma MEN chee SORE uss
Megalosaurus	MEG ah loh SORE uss
Mei long	may LOONG
Microraptor	MY kro RAP tor
Monolophosaurus	MON o LOAF o SORE uss
Muttaburrasaurus	MUT a BUR a SORE uss
Nigersaurus	nee ZHER SORE uss
Ornithomimus	OR ni thoh MEE mus
Ouranosaurus	OO ran oh SORE uss
Oviraptor	oh vee RAP tor
Pachycephalosaurus	PACK ee SEFF allo SORE uss
Pachyrhinosaurus	PACK ee RYE no SORE uss
Parasaurolophus	PA ra SORE oh LOAF uss
Pentaceratops	PEN ta SERRA tops
Plateosaurus	PLAT ee oh SORE uss
Polacanthus	pol a KAN thuss
Protoceratops	PRO toe SERRA tops
Psittacosaurus	Si tak oh SORE uss
Saltasaurus	SAHL tah SORE uss
Sauropelta	SORE oh PEL ta
Scelidosaurus	SKEL i doe SORE uss
Sinornithosaurus	SIGN or nith o SORE uss
Sinosauropteryx	SIGN o saw ROP terricks
Sinraptor	sign RAP tor
Spinosaurus	SPY no SORE uss
Stegoceras	STEG o SER ass
Stegosaurus	steg o SORE uss
Styracosaurus	sty RACK oh SORE uss
Tarbosaurus	TAHR bo SORE uss
Tenontosaurus	te NON to SORE uss
Therizinosaurus	THER i ZIN o SORE uss
Triceratops	try SERRA tops
Troodon	TROH o don
Tyrannosaurus	tie RAN o SORE uss
Velociraptor	vell OSS ee RAP tor
Vulcanodon	vul KAN o don

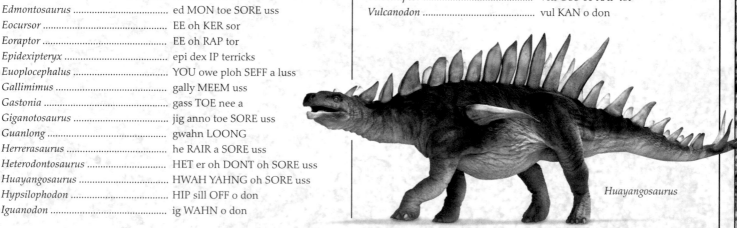

Huayangosaurus

Discovery timeline

IN THE CENTURIES SINCE THE FIRST discovery of dinosaur bones in the 1600s, fossil hunters have unearthed and named dinosaurs in more than 600 different genera. Each find reveals something new, helping scientists piece together how dinosaurs moved, fed, fought, bred, and died. This timeline highlights the major milestones in the study of dinosaurs and lists the steps that have led to our current understanding of these extraordinary creatures.

Roy Chapman Andrews (right)
with *Oviraptor* eggs

1677
English museum curator Robert Plot illustrates part of a *Megalosaurus* femur (thigh bone) in a book. He believes it to be part of the thigh bone of a giant man.

1818
Fossil bones found in Connecticut Valley in the US will later prove to be the first discovery of a North American dinosaur—*Anchisaurus*.

1820
Gideon Mantell, a British doctor, begins collecting fossils of a giant reptile that he later names and describes as *Iguanodon*.

William Buckland

1824
Megalosaurus becomes the first dinosaur to receive a scientific name when British geologist William Buckland publishes an account of its fossil jaw.

1834
American geologist Edward Hitchcock starts collecting fossil tracks in Connecticut Valley. He believes they were made by giant birds, but later research reveals they are tracks made by dinosaurs.

1842
The name "Dinosauria" appears in print for the first time after British anatomist Sir Richard Owen realizes that three kinds of giant fossil reptiles formed part of a special group.

1853
The first lifesize models of dinosaurs appear in a London park in the UK. They are designed by sculptor Benjamin Waterhouse Hawkins and are made of concrete.

1856
American anatomist Joseph Leidy names *Troodon*—the first American dinosaur to be given a scientific name that is still considered valid.

1859
Dinosaur eggshells are reported for the first time, based on discoveries in the south of France.

1861
German paleontologist Hermann von Meyer describes *Archaeopteryx*, a bird with feathered wings but the teeth and bony tail of a dinosaur.

1877
Huge fossil bones found in Colorado start a dinosaur rush to the West. By 1890, teams working for rival paleontologists Othniel C. Marsh and Edward Drinker Cope discover the fossils of many of North America's most famous dinosaurs, such as *Allosaurus, Apatosaurus, Camarasaurus, Diplodocus, Ornithomimus, Triceratops,* and *Stegosaurus.*

1878
Belgian coalminers find fossils of dozens of *Iguanodon* at a depth of 1,056 ft (322 m). Paleontologists later use these to make the first reconstructions of whole dinosaur skeletons.

1887
British paleontologist Harry Govier Seeley splits dinosaurs into two main groups, which he calls the Saurischia (lizard-hipped) and the Ornithischia (bird-hipped).

1902
American fossil hunter Barnum Brown finds the first *Tyrannosaurus* skeleton in Montana.

1903
American paleontologist Elmer S. Riggs names and describes *Brachiosaurus*, two years after fossils of this giant, giraffelike sauropod were discovered in Colorado.

1908–1912
German paleontologists Werner Janensch and Edwin Hennig lead expeditions to Tendaguru, Tanzania. They find fossils of Late Jurassic dinosaurs, including *Brachiosaurus* and *Kentrosaurus.*

1912–1917
American dinosaur hunter Charles Sternberg and his sons collect a wealth of dinosaur fossils in Alberta, Canada, for Canada's Geological Survey.

1915
German paleontologist Ernst Stromer von Reichenbach names the 55¾ ft (17 m) long *Spinosaurus.*

1922–1925
Roy Chapman Andrews, Henry Fairfield Osborn, and Walter Granger lead American expeditions to Mongolia. They find fossils of dinosaurs including *Oviraptor, Protoceratops,* and *Velociraptor,* and discover nests with dinosaur eggs.

1927
In Algeria, French paleontologists Charles Depéret and J. Savornin discover the teeth of a large theropod later named *Carcharodontosaurus.*

1933–1970s
Chinese paleontologist Yang Zhongjian oversees dinosaur fossil discoveries in China and names dinosaurs including *Lufengosaurus, Mamenchisaurus, Omeisaurus,* and *Tsintaosaurus.*

1941
American paleontologist Roland T. Bird describes fossil footprints in Texas made by 12 sauropods walking together. This is the first indication that some dinosaurs traveled in herds.

1951
British paleontologist Kenneth Kermack questions the popular notion that sauropods needed water to buoy up their heavy bodies. He shows that water pressure would have suffocated a snorkeling sauropod.

Carcharodontosaurus skull compared with human skull

1954
Russian paleontologist Evgeny Maleev discovers the enormously long claws of *Therizinosaurus*, later found to be one of a strange group of plant-eating theropods called therizinosaurs.

1965
British paleontologist Alan Charig figures out how dinosaurs, with their upright stance and gait, evolved from sprawling reptiles.

1969
American paleontologist John Ostrom argues that dinosaurs' erect limbs meant that they were active, warm-blooded animals. He claims that birds evolved from small theropods. Ostrom bases these claims largely on his discovery in 1964 of the agile theropod *Deinonychus*.

1971
A Polish-Mongolian expedition in Mongolia finds skeletons of a *Velociraptor* and *Protoceratops* locked in battle.

1972
American paleontologist Robert Bakker suggests that air sacs in some dinosaurs reveal that these must have had a breathing system like that of birds. Later research supports this idea, at least for saurischian (lizard-hipped) dinosaurs.

1974
Paleontologists Peter Galton and Robert Bakker publish a paper where they argue that birds are dinosaurs. Subsequent research provides strong support for their claim.

Robert Bakker

1978
In Montana, American paleontologists John "Jack" Horner and Robert Makela begin excavations of fossil hadrosaur nests, eggs, and young. They find the first evidence that dinosaurs cared for their young.

1979
American geologist Walter Alvarez and his nuclear physicist father Luis Alvarez establish that a large asteroid smashed into Earth at the end of the Cretaceous Period with devastating effects. This was perhaps responsible for killing off all dinosaurs except the birds.

1980
American paleontologist Ralph Molnar describes the first dinosaur discovery from New Zealand—a theropod bone found by amateur fossil hunter Joan Wiffen.

1981
Australian paleontologist Alan Bartholomai and American paleontologist Ralph Molnar describe the ornithopod *Muttaburrasaurus* from the first nearly complete dinosaur skeleton found in Australia.

1984
British paleontologist Michael Benton coins the name "Dinosauromorpha" for the group of reptiles consisting of dinosaurs and their closest relatives.

1986
British paleontologists Alan Charig and Angela Milner describe *Baryonyx*, a fish-eating theropod found in southern England and later identified as a relative of *Spinosaurus*.

1991
American paleontologist William Hammer excavates *Cryolophosaurus*. This crested theropod will become the first Antarctic dinosaur to be named and described in a scientific paper, in 1994.

1993
Argentinian paleontologists José Bonaparte and Jaimé Powell describe the immense sauropod *Argentinosaurus*, possibly the largest dinosaur ever.

American paleontologist Paul Sereno describes *Eoraptor*, the earliest dinosaur to be discovered so far.

Jurassic Park's animatronics and computer simulations set new standards for the lifelike depiction of dinosaurs in films.

1995
Argentinian paleontologists Rodolfo Coria and Leonardo Salgado describe *Giganotosaurus*, a theropod perhaps larger than *Tyrannosaurus*.

1998
Chinese paleontologists Chen Pei-ji, Dong Zhi-ming, and Zhen Shuo-nan name *Sinosauropteryx*, the first known dinosaur with skin covered in downy "dinofuzz" rather than reptilian scales. The discovery supports the theory that birds evolved from theropods.

American paleontologist Karen Chin describes tyrannosaur fossil dung containing bones from a horned dinosaur's skull.

2003
Six Chinese paleontologists describe *Microraptor gui*, a small theropod with feathered arms and legs that helped it to glide from tree to tree.

Sinosauropteryx

American paleontologists Raymond Rogers, David Krause, and Kristina Curry Rogers show that the big Madagascan theropod *Majungatholus* ate others of its kind. This is the first undisputed proof that some dinosaurs were cannibals.

2005
Chinese paleontologists Meng Jin and Wang Yuanqing show that some mammals atc baby dinosaurs. They found fossils of a baby psittacosaur inside a fossil specimen of *Repenomamus robustus*, an opossum-sized mammal that lived in Early Cretaceous China.

Swedish scientist Caroline Strömberg shows that some sauropods fed on grass in Late Cretaceous India. Before this, people thought that no grass existed in the Age of Dinosaurs.

2007
American and Japanese paleontologists report the first real evidence that some dinosaurs lived in burrows. They found fossils of an ornithopod in an underground den. Known as *Oryctodromeus* ("digging runner"), this ornithopod lived in Montana, late in the Cretaceous Period.

2008
Belgian paleontologist Pascal Godefroit and colleagues show that late in the Cretaceous Period, ornithischian (bird-hipped) dinosaurs and theropods not only lived but also bred in Arctic Siberia.

2009
Mary Schweitzer and colleagues at North Carolina State University describe the oldest known protein (body molecule), from an 80-million-year-old hadrosaur's thigh bone. Protein analysis confirms that ornithischian dinosaurs were more closely related to living birds than to alligators.

Paleontologists at an *Argentinosaurus* dig site

Find out more

THERE ARE MORE WAYS OF finding out about dinosaurs than just reading books about these fascinating creatures. Some people join organized fossil hunts. Most of us can study dinosaur skeletons in natural history museums or see exhibitions of lifelike and life-size model dinosaurs that move and make noises. You can also take virtual museum tours on the Internet. Then there are dinosaur films and television documentaries, many of them available as DVDs. Often, these feature scarily realistic models and computer-generated images that help you to grasp what life must have been like in the wonderful and terrible Age of Dinosaurs.

HUNTING FOR FOSSILS
Good hunting grounds for dinosaur fossils include rocks below cliffs that are made of sandstone, mudstone, and clay from the Mesozoic Era. These rocks at Lyme Regis, England, are famous for their fossils of Mesozoic reptiles. Fossil hunters need permission to visit some sites and they should keep away from cliffs where chunks of rock could break off and fall.

GETTING TO KNOW YOU
The fossil dinosaurs you see in a museum are made of bones or copies of bones fitted together and supported by rods. The resulting skeletons stand as the dinosaurs did when alive. Touring exhibitions of skeletons gives you a chance to see fossil dinosaurs from distant parts of the world.

Stegosaurus skeleton at Museum für Naturkunde, Berlin, Germany

Neck is movable

UP CLOSE AND PERSONAL
Some museums offer visitors the chance to watch experts clean a dinosaur fossil still embedded in rock or a plaster jacket. Here, at Pittsburgh's Carnegie Museum of Natural History, children watch paleontologist Alan Tabrum tackle the huge and well-preserved skull of Samson, a *Tyrannosaurus rex*—a two-year task.

Rocks from the Jurassic Period containing dinosaur bones

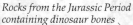

Sled to move the dinosaur

JOIN A DIG!
You might be able to see paleontologists working at a fossil site, or even join in. For years, people have watched experts like this one carefully ease out bones from rock at the Dinosaur National Monument in Utah. Visitors to the Wyoming Dinosaur Center can also go on tours that join paleotechnicians on digs in progress.

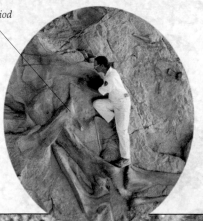

Places to visit

AMERICAN MUSEUM OF NATURAL HISTORY
New York, NY
This major museum features more than
100 specimens in its fossil dinosaur halls.

FIELD MUSEUM OF NATURAL HISTORY
Chicago, IL
The variety of exhibits includes the largest
and best-preserved *Tyrannosaurus*, which is
nicknamed Sue, and the crested theropod
Cryolophosaurus.

NATIONAL MUSEUM OF NATURAL HISTORY
Washington, D.C.
The Smithsonian Institution's huge
collection includes fossils of various
North American dinosaur species.

CARNEGIE MUSEUM OF NATURAL HISTORY
Pittsburgh, PA
The museum has the third-largest show of real
mounted dinosaurs as opposed to casts, and
claims to have the world's largest collection
of Jurassic dinosaurs.

**THE WYOMING DINOSAUR CENTER AND
DIG SITES**
Thermopolis, WY
This large museum is host to more
than 50 active dig sites, which visitors
can tour.

**NATURAL HISTORY MUSEUM OF LOS
ANGELES COUNTY**
Los Angeles, CA
The largest natural and historical museum
in the western United States has a large
collection of dinosaurs.

DINOSAUR VALLEY STATE PARK
Glen Rose, TX
This scenic park on the Paluxy River is home
to some of the best-preserved dinosaur
tracks in the world.

**ROCKY MOUNTAIN DINOSAUR RESEARCH
CENTER**
Woodland Park, CO
The RMDRC features a huge collection of
Late Cretaceous fossils, as well as a working
fossil lab and an interactive children's
learning center.

PEABODY MUSEUM OF NATURAL HISTORY
New Haven, CT
One of the oldest natural history
museums in the world, the Peabody's
Great Hall of Dinosaurs houses impressive
mounted skeletons and the famous Age
of Reptiles mural.

SAN DIEGO NATURAL HISTORY MUSEUM
San Diego, CA
A *Nodosaurus* and a full *Allosaurus*
reconstruction are two of the highlights
of the museum.

**ROYAL TYRRELL MUSEUM OF
PALAEONTOLOGY**
Drumheller, Alberta, Canada
Forty mounted skeletons, mainly of Late
Cretaceous dinosaurs from North America,
make this one of the greatest of all museums
devoted to these animals.

REAL ON REEL

A *Velociraptor* pack threatens a
man in this scene from *Jurassic
Park III* (2001). With their
computer-generated dinosaur
images and robotic models, the
movies in the *Jurassic Park* series
were the first to make dinosaurs
look lifelike, even though they
might not have accurately
represented the actual dinosaurs.
Earlier movies used unconvincing
models, puppets, or lizards with
horns stuck on their heads.

WALKING WITH DINOSAURS

People can now enjoy live shows where lifelike
animatronic dinosaurs stomp and roar. Based
on the UK's BBC documentary series of the
same name, *Walking with Dinosaurs* tours
the world with 15 life-size models up to
56 ft (17 m) long and 36 ft (11 m) tall.

*Audience
at the
live show*

Glossary

AMMONITES
An extinct group of mollusks related to squid; with a coiled shell. They lived in Mesozoic seas.

AMPHIBIANS
A group of cold-blooded vertebrates (backboned animals) originating more than 100 million years before the dinosaurs. The young live in fresh water but many transform into land-based adults. Living amphibians include frogs and salamanders.

ANGIOSPERMS
Flowering plants—one of the two main types of land plant that produce seeds (*see also* GYMNOSPERMS). Angiosperm seeds are enclosed by an ovary, which later develops into a fruit. Flowering plants first appeared in the Cretaceous Period and eventually transformed dinosaur habitats. Angiosperms range from grasses and herbs to great broadleaved trees, and include kinds such as magnolias that have changed little since the Cretaceous.

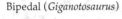

Bipedal (*Giganotosaurus*)

ANKYLOSAURS ("fused lizards")
A group of four-legged, armored, plant-eating ornithischians with bony plates covering the neck, shoulders, and back, and a horny beak used for cropping plants.

ARCHOSAURS
A broad group of extinct and living reptiles with two main subgroups. Crocodiles and their relatives form one group. Dinosaurs, pterosaurs, and their relatives form the other.

ASTEROID
A rocky lump orbiting the Sun. Asteroids are smaller than planets but can measure hundreds of miles across.

BIPEDAL
Walking on two hind limbs, rather than on all fours.

BIRDS
A group of dinosaurs with feathered wings. Some scientists call the whole group Aves. Others call the modern birds Aves or Neornithes, and refer to the extinct, primitive birds as Avialae.

CARNIVORES
Animals that feed on meat.

CARNOSAURS
Large theropods with a big skull and teeth. Once used for all such meat-eaters, the name is now restricted to *Allosaurus* and some of its relatives.

CERATOPSIANS ("horned faces")
Bipedal and quadrupedal, plant-eating ornithischians, with a deep beak and a bony frill at the back of the skull. Many, such as *Triceratops*, had facial horns.

COLD-BLOODED
Animals that are cold-blooded (or more properly, ectothermic), are dependent upon the Sun's heat for body warmth. Most reptiles are cold-blooded (*see also* WARM-BLOODED).

CONIFER
Cone-bearing tree such as a pine or fir.

COPROLITE
Fossilized dung.

CRETACEOUS PERIOD
Third period of the Mesozoic Era; about 145–65 million years ago.

CYCAD
Palm-shaped, seed-bearing plant with long, fernlike leaves. A type of gymnosperm. Cycads were common during the Age of Dinosaurs.

DROMAEOSAURIDS ("running lizards")
A group of birdlike theropods that were closely related to birds.

DUCK-BILLED DINOSAURS
See HADROSAURS

EMBRYO
A plant, animal, or other organism in an early stage of development, before germination, hatching, or birth.

EVOLUTION
The gradual changes in living organisms that occur over many generations, controlled mainly by the process of natural selection (organisms

Mammal (*Negabaata*)

well adapted to their environment produce more offspring than those less well adapted, and pass on more genes to future generations). When populations become separated, they begin evolving independently in different directions, and new species emerge. Dinosaurs gradually evolved from reptile ancestors, and birds evolved, step-by-step, from dinosaurs.

EXTINCTION
The dying-out of a plant or animal species.

FOSSIL
The remains of something that once lived, preserved in rock. Teeth and bones are more likely to form fossils than softer body parts, such as internal organs.

GASTROLITH
Any stone swallowed by an animal to help grind up food in the stomach.

GENUS (plural, **GENERA**)
In the classification of living organisms, a group of closely related species. The species *Tyrannosaurus rex* is grouped with related species into the genus *Tyrannosaurus*.

GINKGO
A unique type of broadleaved tree that evolved in the Triassic Period and survives essentially unchanged to this day. A type of gymnosperm.

GYMNOSPERMS
One of the two main types of land plant that produce seeds. It includes cycads, ginkgos, and conifers, such as pine and fir. Gymnosperms produce naked seeds.

HADROSAURS ("bulky lizards")
Duck-billed dinosaurs. Large, bipedal and quadrupedal ornithopods from late in the Cretaceous Period. They had a ducklike beak that was used for browsing on vegetation.

HERBIVORES
Animals that feed on plants.

ICHTHYOSAURS
Large prehistoric reptiles with a pointed head, flippers, and a tail like a fish's. Ichthyosaurs were streamlined for swimming fast in the sea. Most lived in the Jurassic Period.

JURASSIC PERIOD
Second period of the Mesozoic Era; about 200–145 million years ago.

MAMMALS
Warm-blooded, hairy vertebrates that suckle their young. Mammals began to appear in the Triassic Period.

Cycad

MANIRAPTORANS ("grasping hands")
A group of theropod dinosaurs with long arms and hands, including dromaeosaurids such as *Velociraptor*, and birds.

MESOZOIC ("middle life")
The geological era, about 250–65 million years ago, containing the Triassic, Jurassic, and Cretaceous periods. From the late Triassic on, dinosaurs were the dominant land animals in the Mesozoic.

MOLLUSKS
Snails, clams, squid, and their relatives. Ammonites belonged with the squid and their kin in a group of mollusks called cephalopods.

MOSASAURS
Large aquatic lizards with paddle-shaped limbs and a tail flattened from side to side. They hunted fish and other sea creatures in the Cretaceous Period.

Paleozoic Era (Trilobite fossil)

ORNITHISCHIANS ("bird hips")
One of the two main dinosaur groups (*see also* SAURISCHIANS). In ornithischians, the pelvis (hip bone) is similar to that of birds. Ornithischians include stegosaurs, ankylosaurs, ceratopsians, pachycephalosaurs, and ornithopods.

ORNITHOPODS ("bird feet")
A group of plant-eating, mainly bipedal ornithischians with long hind limbs. The group includes *Iguanodon* and hadrosaurs.

PACHYCEPHALOSAURS
("thick-headed lizards") A group of bipedal ornithischians with a thick skull.

PALEONTOLOGIST
Someone who conducts scientific studies of the fossil remains of plants and animals.

PALEONTOLOGY
The scientific study of fossilized organisms.

PALEOZOIC ("ancient life")
The geological era before the Mesozoic. It lasted from 540 until 250 million years ago and contains the Cambrian, Ordovician, Silurian, Devonian, Carboniferous, and Permian periods.

PLESIOSAURS
A group of large marine reptiles living in the Mesozoic Era, with flipper-shaped limbs and, often, a long neck.

PREDATOR
An animal or plant that preys on animals for food.

PROSAUROPODS ("before sauropods")
A group of early plant-eating saurischians that lived from late in the Triassic Period to early in the Jurassic Period.

PSITTACOSAURS ("parrot lizards")
Bipedal ceratopsians living in the Cretaceous Period. Psittacosaurs had deep beaks like those of parrots and used them to eat plants.

PTEROSAURS ("winged lizards")
Flying reptiles of the Mesozoic Era, related to the dinosaurs.

QUADRUPEDAL
Walking on all fours.

RADIOACTIVE ELEMENT
A substance that decays by giving off particles and energy. Certain elements decay at a known rate. By measuring the radioactivity level of a sample of an element, scientists can work out the age of the sample. Scientists find the age of fossil-bearing rocks by measuring the radioactivity of certain elements that occur in volcanic rocks formed just above or below the fossil-bearing rocks.

REPTILES
Typically, cold-blooded, scaly vertebrates laying eggs or giving birth on land. Living reptiles include lizards, snakes, turtles, and crocodiles.

SAURISCHIANS ("lizard hips")
One of two main dinosaur groups (*see also* ORNITHISCHIANS). In typical saurischians, the pelvis (hip bone) is similar to that of lizards. Saurischians include prosauropods, sauropods, and theropods.

SAUROPODS ("lizard feet")
Huge, quadrupedal, plant-eating saurischians, with long necks and tails. They lived through most of the Mesozoic Era.

SCUTE
Bony plate with a horny covering, set into the skin to protect from an enemy's teeth and claws.

SEDIMENT
Material such as sand and mud deposited by wind, water, or ice.

Trace fossil (coprolite)

SKULL
The head's bony framework protecting the brain, eyes, ears, and nasal passages.

SPECIES
The level below genus in the classification of living things. Individuals in a species can breed to produce fertile young. Each species has a two-part name—*Microraptor gui*, for instance.

STEGOSAURS ("plated/roofed lizards")
Plant-eating, quadrupedal ornithischians with two tall rows of bony plates running down the neck, back, and tail.

THEROPODS ("beast feet")
Mostly predatory saurischians with sharp teeth and claws.

TRACE FOSSIL
The remains of signs of prehistoric creatures, rather than fossils of the creatures themselves, preserved in rock. Trace fossils include footprints, bite marks, droppings, eggs, and fossil impressions of skin, hair, and feathers.

TRIASSIC PERIOD
First period of the Mesozoic Era; about 250–200 million years ago.

TYRANNOSAURIDS ("tyrant lizards")
Huge, bipedal theropods with a large head, short arms, two-fingered hands, and massive hind limbs. Tyrannosaurids flourished late in the Cretaceous Period in North America and Asia.

Sauropod (*Mamenchisaurus*)

WARM-BLOODED
Keeping the body at constant temperature (often above that of the surroundings) by turning energy from food into heat. Warm-blooded animals are more properly called endothermic. Many dinosaurs were probably warm-blooded, although modern reptiles are not. Mammals and birds are warm-blooded (*see also* COLD-BLOODED).

VERTEBRATES
Animals with a spinal column, or backbone.

Index

Acknowledgments

Dorling Kindersley would like to thank:
Sarah Owens for proofreading; Helen Peters for the index; David Ekholm JAlbum, Sunita Gahir, Jo Little, Sue Nicholson, Jessamy Wood, and Bulent Yusuf for the clipart; Sue Nicholson and Jo Little for the wallchart; and Camilla Hallinan for advice.

The Publishers would like to thank the following for their kind permission to reproduce their photographs:

(Key: a-above; b-below/bottom; c-center; l-left; r-right; t-top)

Alamy Images: Katewarn Images 18l (Limestone 2), 18l (Limestone); The Natural History Museum, London 61c, 61tl; vario images GmbH & Co. KG 68cra; **Corbis:** James L. Amos 57cr; Atlantide Phototravel 62bl; Tom Bean 53tr; Bettmann 21cr, 66tr; Jonathan Blair 2cla, 17tr; Gray Braasch 25br (Background); Frank Lane Picture Agency/Derek Hall 68tl; D. Robert & Lorri Franz 28bc; Mark A. Johnson 31bc; Steve Kaufman 18l (Sandstone); Bob Krist 22tl; George D. Lepp 45cr; Louie Psihoyos 28-29c, 46tl, 59br, 60cra, 62tl, 66br, 67cl, 68bc; Louie Psiyoyos 18tr; Nick Rains 43bl; Roger Ressmeyer 39br; Reuters/Charles Platiau 31cr; Pete Saloutos 35br (Ground Ferns); Kevin Schafer 12cl, 19tl; Science Faction/Louie Psihoyos 43cla, 45tl; Sygma/Vo Trung Dung 61tr; Zefa/Murat Taner 36cl (Crane); **DK Images:** Courtesy of The American Museum of Natural History/Lynton Gardiner 6bl, 19tr, 41tr, 59t; Bedrock Studios 57bl; Bedrock Studios/Jon Hughes 17bc, 47l; Robert L. Braun -

Modelmaker/Tim Ridley 14br; Courtesy of the Carnegie Museum of Natural History, Pittsburgh, 18l (Limestone); Centaur Studios - Modelmaker/Andy Crawford 48bl (Baryonyx); Centaur Studios - Modelmakers/Andy Crawford 23bl; David Donkin - Modelmaker/Andy Crawford 12tl, 14tl; Davin Donkin - Modelmaker/Andy Crawford 10tl; ESPL - Modelmaker/Geoff Brightling 25tc; Graham High - Modelmaker/Gary Ombler 37cra; Graham High at Centaur Studios - Modelmaker/Andy Crawford 36cl (Dinosaur); Graham High at Centaur Studios - Modelmaker/Dave King 23br, 47bc, 49c; John Holmes - Modelmaker/Andy Crawford 33tl; John Holmes - Modelmaker/Steve Gorton 43br; Jon Hughes 15clb (Mososaur), 17br, 24bl, 24br; Jeremy Hunt at Centaur Studios - Modelmaker/Dave King 9tr, 41br; Courtesy of the Museo Argentino De Cirendas Naturales, Buenos Aires 54bl; Courtesy of the Natural History Museum, London 52bl; Courtesy of the Natural History Museum, London/Colin Keates 2tr, 4bl, 4cl, 8c, 20cl, 30tl, 34cb, 34cl, 35ca, 39tr, 41clb, 46bl, 47tr (Diplodocus), 49cl, 51tr, 52-53tc, 55c, 55t, 60-61b, 62cl, 62-63cbc; Courtesy of the Natural History Museum, London/John Downes 2b, 20b, 58br; Courtesy of the Natural History Museum, London/John Holmes - Modelmaker/Andy Crawford 33tl; Courtesy of the Natural History Museum, London/Philip Dowell 57br; Courtesy of the Naturmuseum Senckenberg, Frankfurt/Andy Crawford 25tl; Courtesy of Oxford University Museum of Natural History/Richard Hammond - Modelmaker/Steve Gorton 24cla; Peabody Museum of Natural History, Yale

University. All rights reserved/Lynton Gardiner 49br; Luis Rey 24tl (Panderichthys); Courtesy of the Royal Museum of Scotland, Edinburgh/Harry Taylor 19br; Courtesy of the Royal Tyrell Museum of Paleontology, Alberta, Canada/Andy Crawford 51tc; Courtesy of the Royal Tyrell Museum/Andy Crawford 55bl; Courtesy of the Royal Tyrrell Museum of Paleontology, Alberta, Canada/Andy Crawford 26c, 28bl; Courtesy of the Senckenberg Nature Museum, Frankfurt/Andy Crawford 47tr (Elephant); Courtesy of Staatliches Museum für Naturkunde, Stuttgart/Andy Crawford 1, 32cl; Courtesy of the State Museum of Nature, Stuttgart/Andy Crawford 58tl; **Getty Images:** AFP/Hector Mata 45c; Brad Barket 69b; The Bridgeman Art Library 21br; Gallo Images/Travel Ink 19cr; Robert Harding World Imagery/Jochen Schlenker 9br (Background); Hulton Archive 21tl; The Image Bank/Doug Allan 24tl (Background); National Geographic/Ira Block 34tl; National Geographic/Jeffrey L. Osborn 8-9c, 29tr, 45tr; Spencer Platt 6cr; Stocktrek Images 17tl; Stone/G. Brad Lewis 16tl; Stone/Tim Flach 4tr, 54tl; Stringer/Jeff Swensen 68clb; Taxi/Carl Roessler 15clb (Background); Tetra Images 48bl (Water); Visuals Unlimited/Ken Lucas 64-65 (Background), 66-67 (Background), 68-69 (Background), 70-71 (Background), 71cl; **The Kobal Collection:** Amblin/Universal/ILM - Industrial Light & Magic 69ca; Columbia Tristar 23tl; Dreamworks/Paramount 16b; **Mateus:** 49tr; **The Natural History Museum, London:** 20cr, 20tl, 21tr, 26br, 33br, 34bc, 38bl, 50tl, 55cc, 56cl, 56cr, 64tr; Berislav Krzic 29cr; John Sibbick 27br; **Photolibrary:** Mickey Gibson 18l

(Shale 2), 18l (Shale); C.C. Lockwood 18l (Limestone 3); Oxford Scientific/Jen & Des Bartlett 50br; **Rex Features:** Sipa Press 60tl; **Royal Saskatchewan Museum, Canada:** 2crb, 33tr; **Science Photo Library:** Christian Darkin 23ca; Geological Survey of Canada/Mark Pilkington 17cla; Carlos Goldin 67br; Roger Harris 36br; Sheila Terry 66cl; **Still Pictures:** Biosphoto/Jean-Philippe Delobelle 52cl; **Nobumichi Tamura:** 57c.

Wallchart: Corbis: Louie Psihoyos (Triceratops), (Palaeontologist); **DK Images:** Courtesy of The American Museum of Natural History/Lynton Gardiner (Edmontosaurus Mummy); Courtesy of the Natural History Museum, London/John Downes (Nest); Courtesy of Staatliches Museum für Naturkunde, Stuttgart/Andy Crawford (Allosaurus Skull); **Getty Images:** Gallo Images/Travel Ink (Footprint); National Geographic/Ira Block (Nigersaurus); **The Kobal Collection:** Dreamworks/Paramount (Deep Impact).

All other images © Dorling Kindersley
For further information see: www.dkimages.com